VISUAL GUITAR THEORY

by Chad Johnson

ISBN 978-1-4950-8896-4

7777 W. BLUEMOUND RD. P.O. BOX 13819 MILWAUKEE, WI 53213

In Australia Contact:
Hal Leonard Australia Pty. Ltd.
4 Lentara Court
Cheltenham, Victoria, 3192 Australia
Email: ausadmin@halleonard.com.au

Visit Hal Leonard Online at
www.halleonard.com

TABLE OF CONTENTS

ABOUT THE AUTHOR

Chad Johnson is a freelance author, editor, and musician. For Hal Leonard Corporation, he's authored over 75 instructional books covering a variety of instruments and topics, including *Guitarist's Guide to Scales Over Chords*, *How to Fingerpick Songs on Guitar*, *How to Build Guitar Chops*, *Play Like Eric Johnson*, *How to Record at Home on a Budget*, *Bassist's Guide to Scales Over Chords*, and *Ukulele Aerobics*, to name but a few. He's a featured instructor on the DVD *200 Country Guitar Licks* (also published by Hal Leonard) and has toured and performed throughout the East Coast in various bands, sharing the stage with members of Lynyrd Skynyrd, the Allman Brothers Band, and others. He works as a session instrumentalist, composer/songwriter, and recording engineer when not authoring or editing and is working overtime to introduce his two children to the great music of days gone by. Currently residing in Denton, TX (North Dallas) with his family, Chad can be reached at *chadjohnsonguitar@gmail.com* with any questions or concerns.

ACKNOWLEDGMENTS

I'd like to thank my editors for their assistance in the creation and realization of this method. I'd also like to thank everyone at Hal Leonard Corporation for their combined efforts in turning this manuscript into a finished product.

I'd like to acknowledge the brilliant artistry of the late, great Ted Greene, whose outstanding book *Chord Chemistry* did so much for my understanding of harmony in my formative years. (With that beard on the cover, you knew he was a force to be reckoned with!)

I'd also like to give thanks to the music department at the University of North Texas, which helped transform me from simply a "guitar player who knew some cool licks" into an actual musician.

INTRODUCTION

Welcome to *Visual Guitar Theory*. With this book, I aim to expand the beginning or intermediate player's reach by "connecting the dots," so to speak, of the guitar fretboard. Although many players spend years, or entire lives, feeling their way around the neck in the dark, it doesn't have to be that way. Experiencing the freedom that comes with a little theoretical knowledge is not as difficult as it may seem.

The problem is that many people are turned off by music theory because it sounds too technical, uses complicated-sounding jargon, etc. If you're more of a visual learner (i.e., if you prefer to watch a video demonstration rather than read a manual), the idea of learning theory can seem like sitting in a classroom and listening to a lecture on a subject that you don't even find interesting. And that's a shame, because a whole wide world awaits the player who manages to learn a bit of theory.

That's where *Visual Guitar Theory* comes in. The emphasis here is not on a lot of technical jargon, but instead on visual concepts relative to the guitar that will help ease the transition between a "hunt and peck" player and a "play what you hear in your head" player. There are over 500 fretboard diagrams in this book that will help you recognize the all-important concepts that make music work. What's more, the book has been printed in full color to help make the diagrams as visually effective as possible.

I hope you enjoy studying the book as much as I did writing it. I think it represents a unique way to look at theory while still covering the bases in a fun way. That was my intent, anyway. I hope you'll find it a valuable resource in your musical education.

—Chad Johnson, 2017

HOW TO USE THIS BOOK

Visual Guitar Theory contains nine chapters that cover a variety of topics. It's meant for players with little or no music theory experience. (Note that this does not mean a "beginner player." Some of the most famous players of all time knew little or no theory.) To this end, it begins at a fundamental level and progresses throughout the book. Therefore, it's imperative that you work through the book from beginning to end and not skip around. This is especially true for this book because there are systems I use to convey information—color-coding, terms, etc.—that will only make sense if you work from beginning to end.

At the end of each chapter, there's a short quiz to test your retention. I recommend that you don't proceed to the next chapter unless you're able to answer these questions correctly. If necessary, feel free to review the chapter before taking the quiz. (The answers to the quizzes are found in the Appendix.) There's also a brief review of the salient points discussed in that chapter to help make sure you're gleaning all there is to learn. This acts as a catchall for any piece of information that wasn't addressed in the quiz.

Throughout the book, you'll see some sidebars entitled "Dig Deeper." If you're the kind of person that just throws a manual to the side and starts twisting knobs and pushing buttons on a new piece of gear to see what it does, you can probably skip over these your first time through the book. If you're like me, however, and, after ordering a piece of gear online, you download the manual and read it cover to cover before the unit even arrives, then you'll probably want to check those out on the first pass. They contain more specific bits of knowledge with regard to the theory and concepts at hand. They're not considered essential at the time—some may consider them a hindrance to their momentum at first—but they should be visited eventually, as they help complete the bigger picture.

With all that said, it's time to dig in. Here we go!

THE OCTAVE AND HOME BASE

We're going to start our journey with a musical *interval*. This term is simply a fancy name for the distance between two musical notes—a musical yardstick, if you will. The interval we're concerned with now is the *octave*.

THE OCTAVE

An octave is the span from one note to the same note in a higher or lower register. For example, if you play your open low (sixth) string and your open high (first) string, you can hear that they're the same note (assuming you're in tune!), but one sounds higher or lower than the other. That's because these *are* the same notes (E, in this case); they're just in different octaves.

Same notes, different octave

The octave has a sound that's very recognizable. Think of the first two notes in the song "Somewhere Over the Rainbow." The note on "**Some**" is followed by the same note an octave higher for "**where.**" Or think of that holiday classic "The Christmas Song." The first two notes of the melody, again, are separated by an octave: "**Chest-nuts** roasting on an open fire…"

On the piano, octaves are easy to recognize because the pattern of white and black keys repeats all the way up the keyboard. Most people can find middle C on the piano. All of the other C notes in different octaves are easy to spot because they all look the same; they're the white keys directly to the left of the pairs of black keys.

First Thing's First

If you don't know the note names on the sixth string yet, head over to the fretboard chart in the Appendix and learn at least the natural notes—the ones without a sharp (♯) or flat (♭)—before proceeding. It won't take long—I promise! But, at this point, it's imperative that you're at least able to locate a note by name on the sixth string.

DIG DEEPER

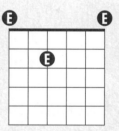

The open E strings on your guitar are actually two octaves apart; there's another E between them, which is located at fret 2 of string 4. (This note can also be played at two other spots on the neck. Can you find them?)

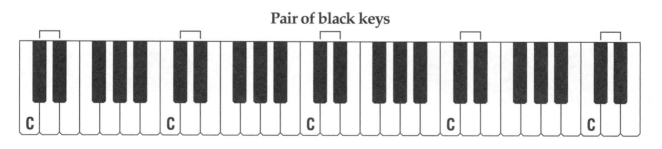

Pair of black keys

This is what makes the piano keyboard such a useful tool when learning theory. It's a great visual representation of what's going on musically. But the guitar neck can be quite visual, as well, as we'll soon see!

HOME BASE SHAPES

On the guitar, octaves create clear, visible shapes that nicely frame portions of scales and chords that we use all the time. In this regard, we can use them as signposts to help navigate the guitar neck. I like to think of these octave shapes as "home base"—in other words, shapes off which you can base various chords, licks, scales, etc. We'll look at two different groups of shapes, which I call *forward-facing* and *backward-facing*.

DIG DEEPER

Why are the forward-facing shapes more commonly used when playing riffs? It's most likely because they're simply easier to play. If you're using a pick to strum the shape, you only have one "in-between" string to deaden, whereas you have two in-between strings to deaden in the backward-facing shapes. It probably also has to do with the fact that you get to anchor the forward-facing shape on the lowest-pitched note with the index finger, which generally feels more natural to most people.

Forward-Facing Octave Shapes

These are the most common octave shapes, so we'll start with them. In a forward-facing octave shape, the higher-pitched note is on a higher fret than the lower-pitched note. We can play them based off the sixth, fifth, fourth, or third strings. Here's how they look on the neck.

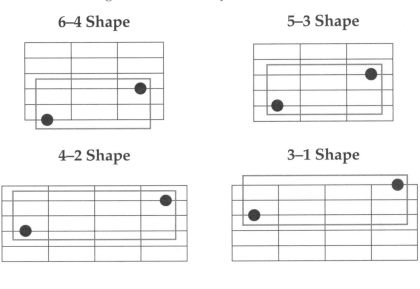

6–4 Shape   5–3 Shape

4–2 Shape   3–1 Shape

Notice that the shapes based off the sixth and fifth strings span two frets, whereas the shapes based off the fourth and third strings span three frets because of the "odd man out" tuning of the B string. Consequently, you should use the index and pinky when playing the 4–2 and 3–1 shapes. For the lower-string shapes, however, you can use the index and ring finger or the index and pinky.

Backward-Facing Octave Shapes

Though not nearly as common as forward-facing octaves, the backward-facing shapes are still extremely important from a visual standpoint. In these shapes, the higher-pitched note is on a lower fret than the lower-pitched note. We can play them based off the sixth, fifth, or fourth strings.

6–3 Shape   5–2 Shape   4–1 Shape

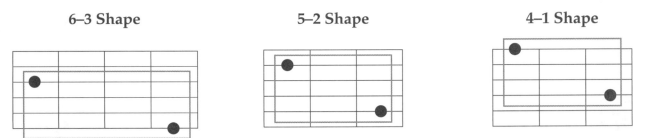

Again, the shapes differ depending on whether or not the B string is involved. The octave spans three frets for the 6–3 shape, while it spans two frets for the 5–2 and 4–1 shapes.

I should mention that these labels—forward-facing and backward-facing—are not in standard use throughout the guitar world. I just find them useful in describing the shapes.

CHORD CONNECTIONS

As mentioned previously, these octave shapes frame important chord forms that we guitar players use all the time. Each open-form chord can be turned into a moveable barre chord form, and each one resides within one (or, in some instances, one and a half) of these octave shapes. If you simply think of the open string as fret zero, you can visualize each open chord as a barre form. Treating each one of these octave shapes as the root of a chord, we can overlay a chord shape and see how they align.
Let's take a look…

E Form

The open E chord has its root on the sixth string, so we'll use the 6–4 octave shape to frame it.

Open E Chord   **Moveable Barre Form**

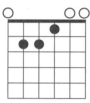 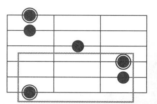

Extra credit: We're just looking at two-note octave shapes here, but can you find another root note in this chord form? If not, check back after reading the forthcoming "Two for the Price of One" section!

A Form

Open A has its root on the fifth string, so it's framed with the 5–3 octave shape.

Open A Chord   **Moveable Barre Form**

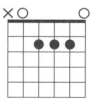 

Note: We used all major chord forms here, but the same root/octave relationship applies to their respective minor forms, as well.

D Form

The open D chord has its root on the fourth string, so it's framed with the 4–2 octave shape.

Open D Chord   **Moveable Barre Form**

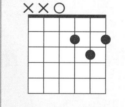 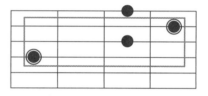

G Form

Open G has its root on the sixth string, but it's a backward-facing chord, so we'll use the 6–3 shape.

Open G Chord   **Moveable Barre Form**

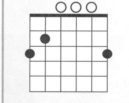 

C Form

Finally, the open C has its root on the fifth string, but it's also a backward-facing chord, so we'll use the 5–2 shape. As you can see, this is the only instance in which the entire chord is not enclosed by the octave shape's fret span. Nevertheless, the octave shape is clearly visible in the form.

Open C Chord   **Moveable Barre Form**

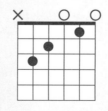 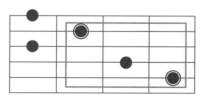

USING OCTAVES TO LEARN THE NOTES ON THE NECK

Another great thing about these octave shapes is that you can use them as a "cheat" to learn the notes all over the guitar neck. Let's check out how this is done.

Two for the Price of One

By now, hopefully you've at least learned the natural notes (i.e., not sharp or flat) on the low E string. There's just no way around this. In order to learn the notes on the neck, you must start by learning the notes on one string, and it may as well be the low E. The great news, though, is that once you learn the notes on string 6 (the low E string), you already know them on string 1! The first string is also an open E; the only difference is that it's two octaves above string 6. But the note names are the same on every single fret. So get used to automatically recognizing this relationship any time you're playing on either one of these strings.

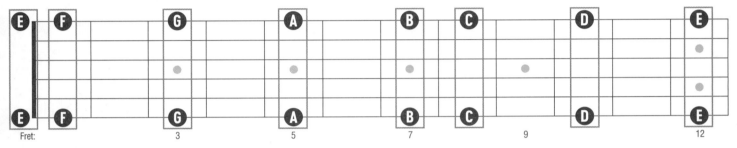

Two Frets Forward, Two Frets Back to Learn the D String

We can bring the fourth string into the mix with the two-frets trick. When moving from string 6 or string 1 to string 4, you count two frets up to find the same note (albeit in a different octave). When moving from string 4 to string 6 or 1, you count two frets back to find the same note. This is equivalent to the forward-facing 6–4 octave shape and the backward-facing 4–1 octave shape.

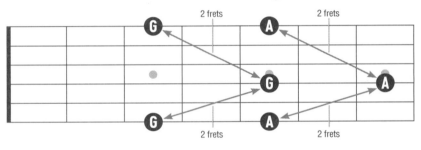

Three Frets Back, Three Frets Forward to Learn the G String

To relate the third string to the E strings, we use the three-frets trick. When moving from string 6 or string 1 to string 3, you count three frets back to find the same note (albeit in a different octave). When moving from string 3 to string 6 or 1, you count three frets forward to find the same note. This is the same as the backward-facing 6–3 octave shape and the forward-facing 3–1 octave shape.

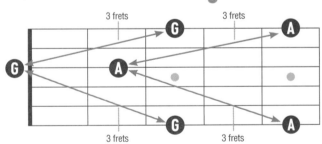

This leaves only the B (second) and A (fifth) strings, but we still have another trick up our sleeve to learn them.

Two Frets Forward, Two Frets Back to Learn the A and B Strings

We can use the G string as our reference for learning the A string, as they have a two-frets relationship. Starting from a note on string 3 and moving to string 5, we move back two frets to find the same note an octave lower. We can then use the A string as a reference for learning the B string with another two-frets relationship. Starting from a note on string 5 and moving to string 2, we move back two frets to find the same note an octave higher. This uses the forward-facing 5–3 octave shape and the backward-facing 5–2 octave shape.

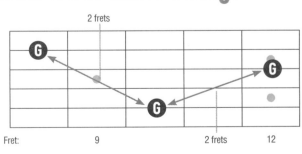

CHAPTER 1 QUIZ

The answers to each chapter quiz can be found in the Appendix. The first example in each section below is done for you.

A. Fill in the Missing Octave Note and Draw a Box Around the Octave Shape

1. Octave higher on string 4.

2. Octave higher on string 2.

3. Octave lower on string 4.

4. Octave lower on string 6.

Identify the Octave Shapes in These Chord Forms by Circling the Roots

1.

2.

3.

4 .

Name the Notes Shown on the Fretboard

1.

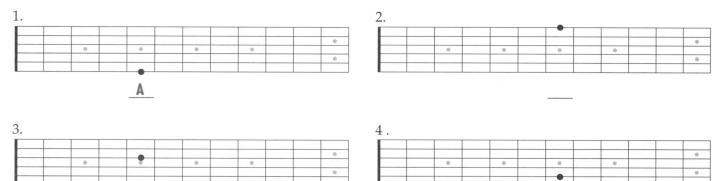

A

2.

3.

4 .

Chapter 1 Review

Before proceeding, make sure you have a good grip on the following:

- You know the names of (at least) the natural notes on the sixth string by memory.
- You know the various forward- and backward-facing octave shapes.
- You can use the octave shapes to figure out the names of the natural notes on all six strings.
- You can identify the root notes (and consequent octave shapes) present in the five different chord forms: E Form, A Form, D Form, G Form, and C Form.

CHAPTER 2
HALF STEPS AND WHOLE STEPS

In this chapter, we're going to learn about two more incredibly useful intervals: the *half step* and the *whole step*. No, these aren't the names of two dance crazes sweeping the nation; they're simply the two smallest "building blocks" that we use in Western music when creating melodies, scales, and chords.

THE HALF STEP

The half step is the smallest musical interval in Western music. On the guitar, it's simply the distance of one fret to the next on any string. All of the following examples are half steps.

Same-String Half Steps

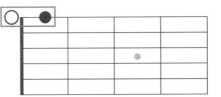

DIG DEEPER

As mentioned, the half step is the smallest interval we have at our disposal. In the Western musical alphabet, we have 12 different notes per octave, including natural and sharp/ flat notes. If you look at a piano keyboard, you'll notice that there are seven white keys and five black keys for every octave. This means that there are two places in each octave where white keys border each other. On the piano, these white keys represent the "natural" notes, while the black keys represent the sharp or flat notes (there are exceptions to this, but you needn't worry about that right now). This means that there are two *natural half steps* in our musical alphabet. These are located from B to C and from E to F.

If you play these shapes in ascending fashion (i.e., the low note first and then the higher note), you'll probably recognize it (if you're old enough, that is!) as the interval that John Williams exploited for the *Jaws* theme.

We can also use two strings to play half steps so that we can allow the notes to ring together if we'd like. Played by themselves, these sound pretty dissonant. But within the context of certain chords, the interval can sound quite nice and striking—still dissonant, but in a pretty way.

Here, then, are the fingerings for half steps on each adjacent string group. Depending on where you are on the neck, they can be quite a stretch, with the 3–2 string pair being one exception.

Adjacent-String Half Steps

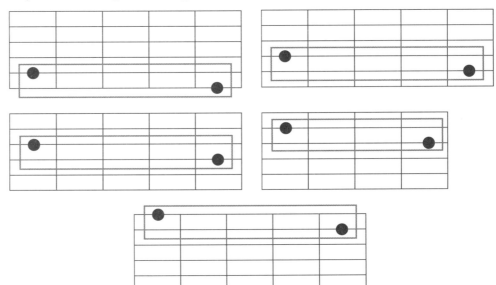

THE WHOLE STEP

As you may suspect, a whole step is twice the size of a half step. On the guitar, it's the distance of two frets on the same string. Compare the intervals below to the same-string half steps that we just covered.

Same-String Whole Steps

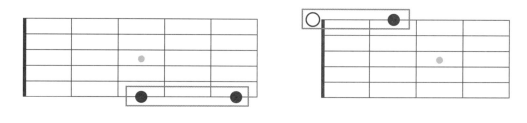

The whole step is another extremely common interval that's heard all the time. The opening guitar riff of "Helter Skelter" by the Beatles is an example of one particularly gritty whole-step interval.

We can play whole steps on adjacent strings, as well. While these sound dense, they're not nearly as dissonant as half steps and therefore are much more common in general. Here's how they look on adjacent string pairs:

Adjacent-String Whole Steps

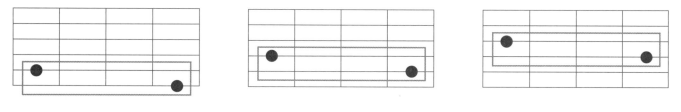

DIG DEEPER

If you've ever heard of suspended chords, or "sus" chords for short, then you're familiar with how a whole step can be used in a chord. In a sus2 chord, for example, a note that's a whole step above the root (which is called the 2nd) is present in the chord. It replaces the middle note of the chord (which is the 3rd) and is responsible for the arid, open sound of the sus chord. We'll talk more about this in upcoming chapters.

LEARNING THE IN-BETWEEN NOTES

When playing the same-string half-step shapes, you may have played some notes for which you didn't know the name because they lay in between two natural notes. So let's remedy that quickly before we move on.

Sharps

A *sharp* note is simply one half step higher than a natural note. If, for example, we move a half step (or one fret) higher than a natural note, we simply add a sharp to that natural note's name.

For example, let's say we have this G note on string 6:

If we move a half step higher, we have a G♯ note:

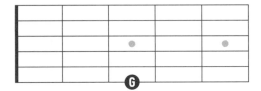

If we have an F note on string 4:

A half step above it is an F♯ note:

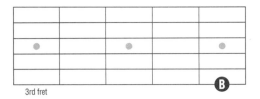

Flats

As you may have intuited, *flats* are simply the opposite of sharps. A flat note is one half step lower in pitch than a natural one. So, if we move a half step (one fret) lower than a natural note, we just add a flat to that natural note's name.

For example, let's say we have this B note on string 6, fret 7:

If we move down one fret, or one half step, we have a B♭ note:

Or let's say we have this D note on string 5, fret 5:

A half step below that, at fret 4, is D♭:

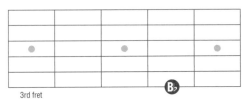

DIG DEEPER

Whereas notes without a sharp or flat are referred to as "natural," sharp and flat notes are referred to as *accidentals*. But don't let the name fool you; there's nothing "accidental" about them, and they're used in all kinds of music all the time.

A NOTE BY ANY OTHER NAME IS STILL THE SAME

Now, if you've been observant, you may have been wondering, "Why is it that the note a half step above G is called G♯, and not A♭?" After all, we said previously that the note a half step below the D note at fret 5, string 5 is D♭. Well, I'm glad you asked! The answer is… it can be both!

The note in between G and A can have two names. It can be called G♯ or A♭, depending on several factors. These include things like the key of the song, the direction of the melody, the current chord being played, etc. At this point, you don't need to worry about that; just realize that every sharp note can also be named a flat note, and vice versa. It just depends on whether you're looking forward or backward. Let's see this idea in action.

String 3, Fret 3

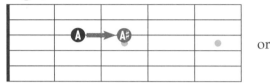 or

DIG DEEPER

The term used to describe two different names for the same note is *enharmonic*. So, we would say that G♭ and F♯ are enharmonic. Or you can say the enharmonic equivalent of D♭ is C♯, etc. Eventually, you'll know why and when a sharp is used instead of a flat, or vice versa. But for now, at least you can impress your friends with a fancy term.

String 5, Fret 4

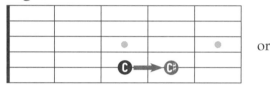 or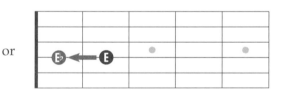

String 1, Fret 2

 or

String 4, Fret 1

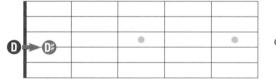 or

NATURAL HALF STEPS

In the musical alphabet, we use seven different note names: A through G. If you look at a piano keyboard and are asked to compare the black and white keys, you'll probably say two things: the black keys are shorter and, more importantly for our purposes, there are **more white keys than black keys**. Another way of saying this is that there are more natural notes than accidentals—two more in each octave, to be exact. There are seven natural notes (white keys on the piano) and five accidental notes (black keys).

This means that there are two spots in each octave where we don't have "in-between notes." This occurs between B and C and between E and F. Here's a demonstration on string 6, along with a keyboard visual:

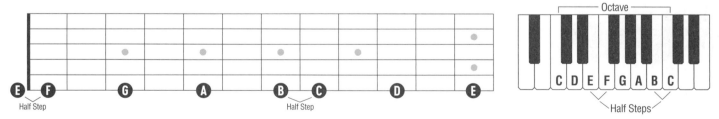

What this means is that we generally don't use note names like C♭, B♯, F♭, or E♯. Those notes would normally be called by their much more common names: B, C, E, and F, respectively. I say "generally" because there *are* some exceptions to this. Sometimes it will make sense to call a note E♯ instead of F, for example, but it's certainly much less common.

CHAPTER 2 QUIZ

The answers to each chapter quiz can be found in the Appendix. The first example in each section below is done for you.

A. Add the Requested Note to the One Shown

1. Same string, half-step higher.

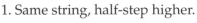

2. Same string, whole-step lower.

3. Adjacent string, whole-step higher.

4. Adjacent string, half-step lower.

5. Adjacent string, half-step higher.

6. Adjacent string, whole-step lower.

B. Identify the Following Intervals as Half Step (HS) or Whole Step (WS)

1.

HS

2.

____

3.

____

4.

____

5.

____

6.

____

C. Name the Missing Note (two possible answers for each)

1.

F# or G♭

2.

____

3.

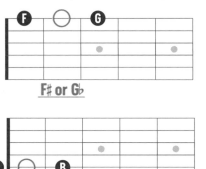

____

4.

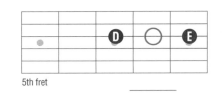

5th fret

____

Chapter 2 Review

Before proceeding, make sure you have a good grip on the following:

- You know what half steps and whole steps look like on one string.
- You know what half steps and whole steps look like on each adjacent string pair.
- You know how sharps and flats relate to natural notes.
- You know where the natural half steps occur in the musical alphabet.
- You can name all 12 notes from the open string to the 12th fret along (at least) the sixth string.

CHAPTER 3
THE MAJOR AND MINOR CONCEPT

We hear the terms "major" and "minor" constantly in music. They're applied to chords and scales of all types, and even songs themselves are considered to be in a major or minor key. In this chapter, we're going to discover the determining factors that make something major or minor and how those concepts apply to the guitar fretboard.

In the last chapter, we looked at half steps and whole steps and how to play them on the fretboard. Now we're going to increase our intervallic reach just a tad and learn about *3rds*. There are two types of 3rds: minor 3rds and major 3rds. Let's examine how these intervals look on the fretboard.

DIG DEEPER

The half step and whole step intervals we looked at in the last chapter also go by other names: minor 2nd and major 2nd, respectively. We'll talk more about this idea as we progress and shed more light on intervals.

MAJOR 3RDS

Let's get the feel of a major 3rd under our fingers and the sound in our ear. Below are several instances of a major 3rd interval on one string.

Same-String Major 3rds

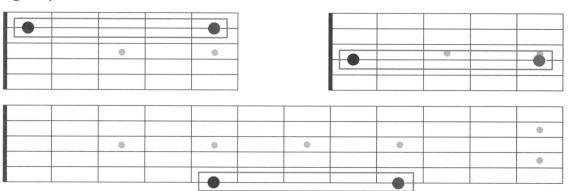

So, we can see that each one spans four frets on the same string. Another way we can look at it is to say that a major 3rd spans the distance of two whole steps (WS).

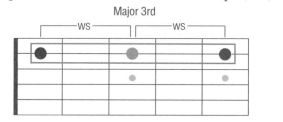

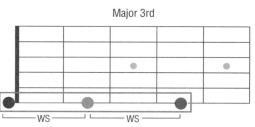

Now let's see at how these shapes look on each adjacent string pair.

Adjacent-String Major 3rds

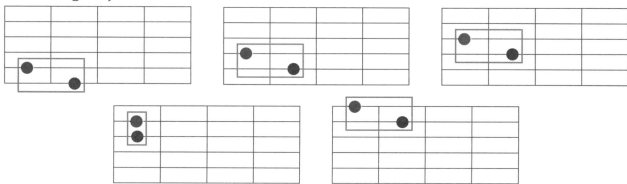

As expected, the shapes are uniform across each string pair, save for the one that involves the B string. Practice playing these shapes both harmonically (notes played together) and melodically (notes played one after the other) and concentrate on the sound they generate.

MINOR 3RDS

Now let's check out some minor 3rds. First, here are some examples of minor 3rd intervals on one string:

Same-String Minor 3rds

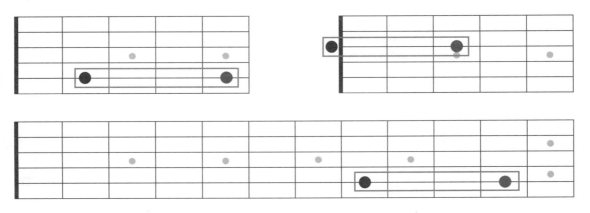

So, whereas a major 3rd spanned four frets on one string, the minor 3rd spans three. Another way we can say it is that a minor 3rd is a combination of a whole step and a half step.

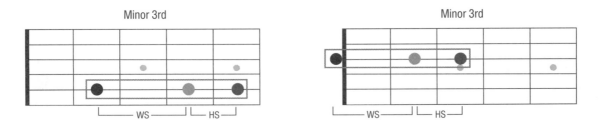

Below are what minor 3rds look like when played on adjacent string pairs. Compare these—in both shape and sound—to the major 3rd shapes.

Adjacent-String Minor 3rds

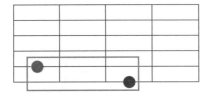  

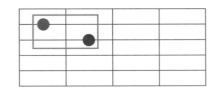 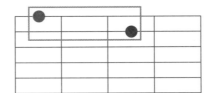

DIG DEEPER

The minor 3rd is the next largest interval beyond the whole step. To review:

- A half step spans one fret on one string.
- A whole step spans two frets on one string.
- A minor 3rd spans three frets on one string.
- A major 3rd spans four frets on one string.

We can also say the following:

- A whole step spans two half steps.
- A minor 3rd spans one whole step plus a half step, or…
- A minor 3rd spans three half steps.
- A major 3rd spans two whole steps, or…
- A major 3rd spans four half steps.

The Major-Minor Relationship

If you've been paying attention, you've probably noticed that all of the major 3rd shapes are one half step larger than the minor 3rd shapes. This is an important concept, and it will play out in many more aspects of music theory. Note the relationship in the following diagrams.

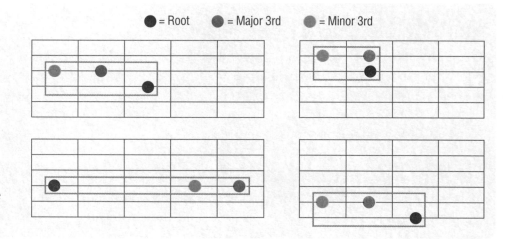

CHORD CONNECTIONS

Just as we saw how the octave shapes fit into the open chord forms, we can do the same with both types of 3rds. In the chord forms below, the major 3rds (contained in major chords) will be red, the minor 3rds (contained in minor chords) will be blue, and the roots will be circled. We'll just look at the moveable forms here.

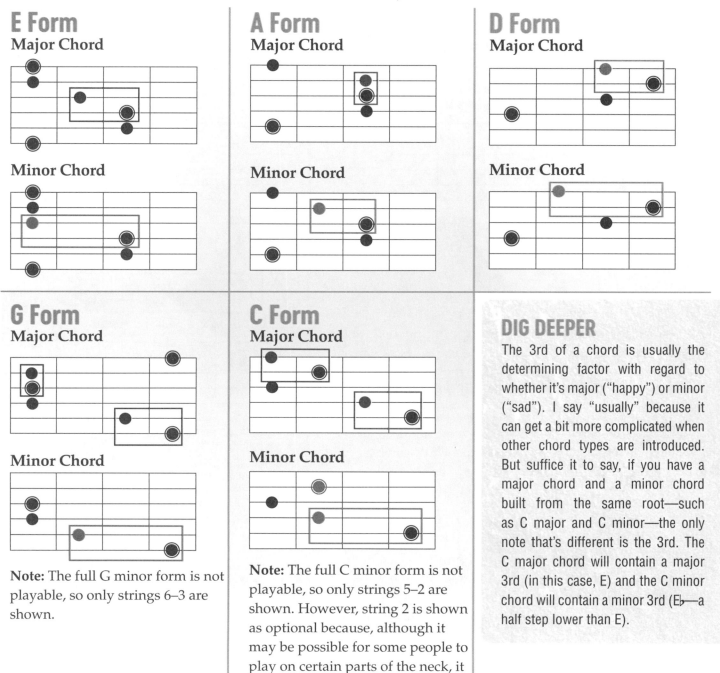

E Form
Major Chord
Minor Chord

A Form
Major Chord
Minor Chord

D Form
Major Chord
Minor Chord

G Form
Major Chord
Minor Chord

Note: The full G minor form is not playable, so only strings 6–3 are shown.

C Form
Major Chord
Minor Chord

Note: The full C minor form is not playable, so only strings 5–2 are shown. However, string 2 is shown as optional because, although it may be possible for some people to play on certain parts of the neck, it certainly doesn't make for a very practical form.

DIG DEEPER

The 3rd of a chord is usually the determining factor with regard to whether it's major ("happy") or minor ("sad"). I say "usually" because it can get a bit more complicated when other chord types are introduced. But suffice it to say, if you have a major chord and a minor chord built from the same root—such as C major and C minor—the only note that's different is the 3rd. The C major chord will contain a major 3rd (in this case, E) and the C minor chord will contain a minor 3rd (E♭—a half step lower than E).

MOVING THE PATTERNS

We've now looked at five different intervals: the octave, the half step, the whole step, the minor 3rd, and the major 3rd. Let's now talk about how the patterns created by these intervals can be transferred to other areas of the neck. For this, we're going to get specific with notes instead of just referring to shapes alone, so if you're still fuzzy on the note names, this will help in that regard, as well. We'll maintain the circled root and color-coding system of 3rds from the previous examples.

Moving Up or Down an Octave While Staying in the Same Position

Let's start by transferring some intervals by an octave without drastically moving out of position. In other words, many people know you can play the same thing an octave higher by moving up 12 frets. But that's not necessary, nor is it always practical, so we need to know another way to do it. By using the different interval shapes we've learned (i.e., same-string shapes, adjacent-string shapes, and forward/backward-facing octave shapes), we've got the tools to do just that.

Let's say we want to move this harmonic (both notes played together) major 3rd G–B shape, which is on strings 6–5, up an octave:

Start by moving the lowest note (the root) up an octave. We have two basically equidistant choices: a forward-facing shape or a backward-facing shape. The forward-facing shape puts the root on string 4, whereas the backward-facing shape puts the root on string 3. With the roots there, we simply add the major 3rd back in. So here are the two possibilities:

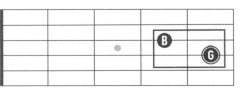

Or let's say we want to move this melodic (notes played one at a time) whole-step interval of A to B up an octave while staying in second position:

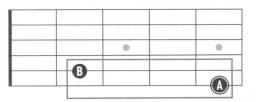

If we use the forward-facing octave shape for the root, we'll be out of second position, so we need to use the backward-facing octave shape, which will put the root on string 3. Then we can use the same-string shape for the whole step.

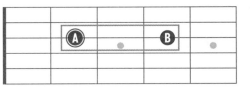

Or how about we move the following melodic minor 3rd E–G shape on strings 2–1 down an octave while staying near second/third position?

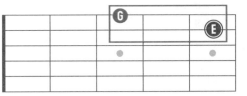

The root is on string 2, fret 5, so moving it down an octave, to string 5, would take us too far out of position. Therefore, we'll move it to string 4, fret 2. In order to stay in second position, and since we don't need to play the two notes together, we'll use a same-string interval shape for the minor 3rd, which looks like this:

Moving the Same Patterns to Different Spots on the Neck

In addition to moving things vertically across the strings to different octaves, it's important to be able to simply move notes to a different spot on the neck while staying in the same octave. This is an essential skill with regard to developing the freedom to move about the neck at will.

To do this, we're going to form a connective chain spanning the length of the fretboard that links together the various shapes on different strings. For this exercise, we're going to assume all of these shapes are melodic intervals (i.e., we don't need to play both notes at once). Let's start with the same E–G minor 3rd shape on strings 2–1 from earlier.

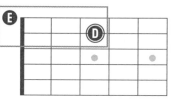

Now, by shifting between adjacent-string and same-string shapes, we can move that minor 3rd all the way up the neck.

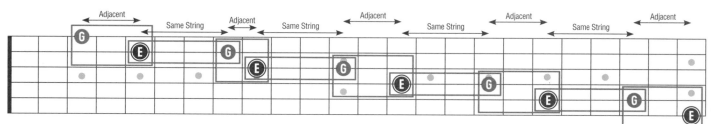

Let's do the same thing for a whole-step interval of D to E:

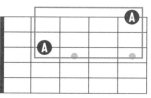

Here's what it looks like when we move the interval across the neck, string by string:

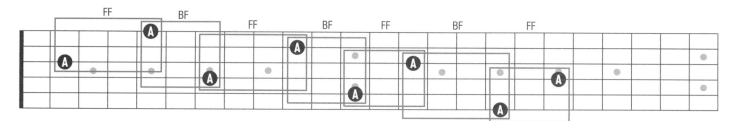

And now let's do the same with this octave shape on the note A:

By alternating between forward-facing (FF) and backward-facing (BF) octave shapes, we can move the shape down the neck:

Of course, don't overlook that fact that these links can be viewed in the opposite direction, as well. For both of the previous diagrams, start on the right side and work backward.

CHAPTER 3 QUIZ

The answers to each chapter quiz can be found in the Appendix. The first example in each section below is done for you.

A. Add the Requested Note to the One Shown

1. Same string, major 3rd higher.

2. Same string, minor 3rd lower.

3. Adjacent string, minor 3rd higher.

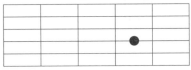

4. Adjacent string, major 3rd lower.

5. Adjacent string, major 3rd higher.

6. Adjacent string, minor 3rd lower.

B. Identify the Following Intervals as Major 3rd (M3) or Minor 3rd (m3)

1.

M3

2.

3.

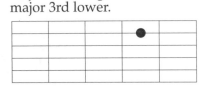

4.

5.

6.

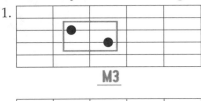
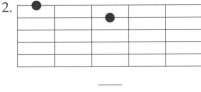
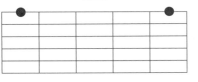

C. Perform the Following Tasks

1. Move the following interval down an octave to the 5–4 string set.

2. Move the following interval down an octave and change to an adjacent-string shape on the 4–3 string set.

3. Move the following interval up an octave to an adjacent-string shape on the 3–2 string set.

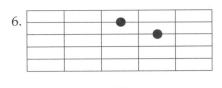

4. Move the following interval to the 4–3 string set.

5. Move the following interval to string 3, using a same-string shape.

6. Move the following interval to the 4–3 string set.

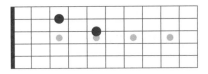

Chapter 3 Review

Before proceeding, make sure you have a good grip on the following:

- You know what major and minor 3rds look like on one string.
- You know what major and minor 3rds look like on each adjacent string pair.
- You understand the relationship between a major and minor 3rd (i.e., a minor 3rd is one half step smaller than a major 3rd).
- You can recognize the major and minor 3rd intervals within the E, A, D, C, and G chord forms.
- You're able to transfer octaves, half steps, whole steps, and 3rds (both types) up or down an octave while staying in the same area on the neck.
- You're able to transfer octaves, half steps, whole steps, and 3rds (both types) to different strings and positions on the neck.

CHAPTER 4
BUILDING TRIADS

A *triad* is the most common type of chord in Western music. Consisting of three different notes (hence the name), it's what people are referring to when they say things like "a C chord" or "a D minor chord" with no other information given. We already know two of the notes needed to build a triad: the root and the 3rd. Now we're going to add the other note.

THE 5TH

The 5th interval is quite likely one of the first intervals many guitarists learn. In fact, another name for a 5th is the *power chord*. Sound familiar? Let's take a look at how they lay out on the different string sets. We won't bother with same-string shapes, as they're not very practical because of the crazy stretch they would create.

Adjacent-String 5ths

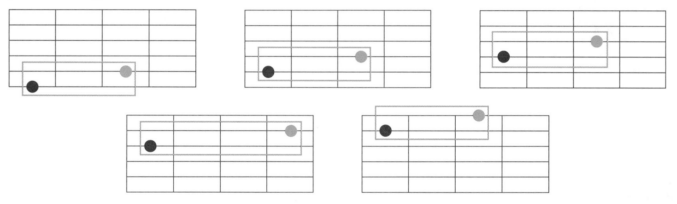

Although we won't look at same-string shapes for 5ths, we do have another possibility besides adjacent-string shapes. These non-adjacent shapes involve skipping one string. This means that, if you strum them with a pick, you're going to have to employ some fret-hand muting to keep the in-between string quiet.

Non-Adjacent-String 5ths

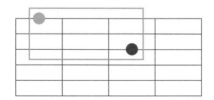

When you play a power chord (root/5th or root/5th/octave root), you're leaving out the 3rd of the triad. This is why power chords sound so open and expansive. They're neither major nor minor because they don't have a 3rd—the determining factor in whether a chord is one or the other.

DIG DEEPER
Why is it called a 5th? Well, it's simply because it's five note names away from the root. For example, a 5th above C is G; we can confirm this by counting through the notes of the musical alphabet: C (1)–D (2)–E (3)–F (4)–G (5). By the same token, a 3rd is simply three note names from the root. The 3rd of C, for example, is E: C (1)–D (2)–E (3). Referred to as the interval's *quantity*, this is one half of the interval story. There are different types of 5ths, but they *always* involve five note names (otherwise, it's technically not a 5th). The same can be said for any interval. A 3rd, whether it's a major or minor 3rd (those are the only two types of 3rds), will *always* involve three note names.

CHORD CONNECTIONS

Now let's see how the 5th interval appears within the five basic chord forms. The 5ths will appear as green dots in these diagrams. Again, as with the 3rds in the previous chapter, we'll only look at the moveable forms here. Notice that we see both adjacent-string 5ths and non-adjacent-string 5ths in these forms; some chord forms even contain both.

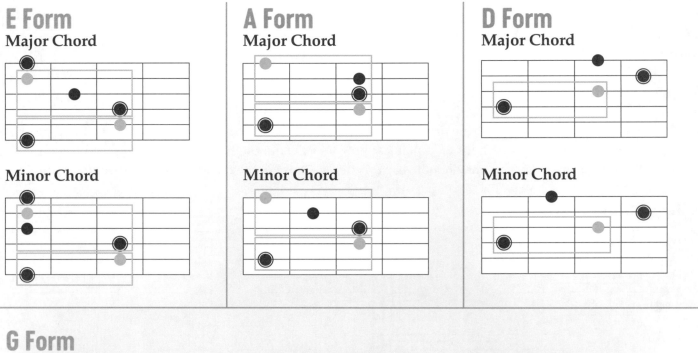

G Form

Major Chord – Version A   **Major Chord – Version B**   **Minor Chord**

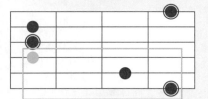

Note: Two versions of the G major form are shown—one with a 3rd and extra root on top, and one with only a 5th on top. The full version of the G minor form is not playable, so only strings 6–3 are shown.

C Form

Major Chord   **Minor Chord**

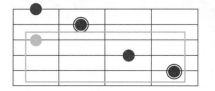

Note: The full C minor form is not playable, so only strings 5–2 are shown. However, string 2 is shown as optional because it's not a very practical form.

Did you notice that the 5ths didn't change at all from major to minor? This helps to underscore the fact that the 3rd alone is the determining factor in whether a chord is major or minor. The roots and 5ths are the same in both.

TRIAD CONSTRUCTION

You should now be familiar with both 3rd (major and minor) and 5th intervals and how they look on the guitar neck. Armed with this knowledge, we can begin looking at various triad shapes and eventually see how they can be moved around the fretboard. The goal is to get to the point where you can play some form of just about any triad without having to move more than one or two frets from any place on the neck.

Of course, you've already been playing triad chords; the full five- and six-string chord forms we've been playing are, in fact, triad chords because they contain only three *different* notes (root, 3rd, and 5th). It's just that some of the notes have been doubled in different octaves to help fill out the chord form. What we're doing here, however, is only using specific three-note voicings so we can quickly see exactly what's going on. This isn't just an exercise, though; these leaner voicings are extremely useful in all kinds of music—from folk and funk to classical and blues, and more!

For now, the root is always going to be the lowest-pitched note in these forms, so every chord will contain, from low to high, a root, 3rd, and 5th (we'll see how we can mix these up in later chapters). We'll maintain the same color scheme from the previous chapters: major 3rds will be red, minor 3rds will be blue, and 5ths will be green. The box will be the color of the 3rd to signify a major chord (red) or a minor chord (blue).

Root on the Sixth String

Major Chord   **Minor Chord**

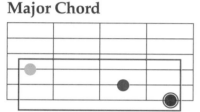

DIG DEEPER

Remember that these chords are in root position because the root is on the bottom. There are other ways we can arrange the three notes of these chords, and we'll look at those ways in upcoming chapters. But for now, we're dealing with all root-position chords.

Root on the Fifth String

Major Chord   **Minor Chord**

Root on the Fourth String

Major Chord   **Minor Chord**

Root on the Third String

Major Chord   **Minor Chord**

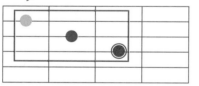

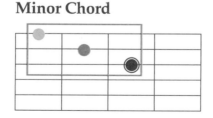

Notice that it's the 5th interval that frames these chords—specifically, the "box" shape created by the root and the 5th.

CHORD CONNECTION

For the sake of being thorough, let's look at our full-version chords now and see if we can spot these specific three-note forms inside them.

E Form

Major Chord   **Minor Chord**

A Form

Major Chord   **Minor Chord**

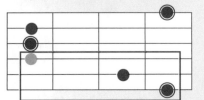

D Form

Major Chord   **Minor Chord**

Note: There aren't any of our three-note triad shapes present in these D Form chords.

G Form

Major Chord   **Minor Chord**

Note: The full version of the G minor form is not playable, so only strings 6–3 are shown.

C Form

Major Chord   **Minor Chord**

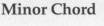

Note: The full C minor form is not playable, so only strings 5–2 are shown.
However, string 2 is shown as optional because it's not a very practical form.

OTHER TRIAD TYPES

Up until now, we've dealt only with major and minor chords because they're by far the most popular. But there are two other types of triads that exist, and we create them by altering the 5th interval.

The ♭5th

The ♭5th interval is one half step *smaller* than the natural 5th (which is also called a *perfect* 5th). Compare the following shapes to see the difference between the perfect 5th (P5) and the ♭5th (♭5).

Adjacent-String 5ths

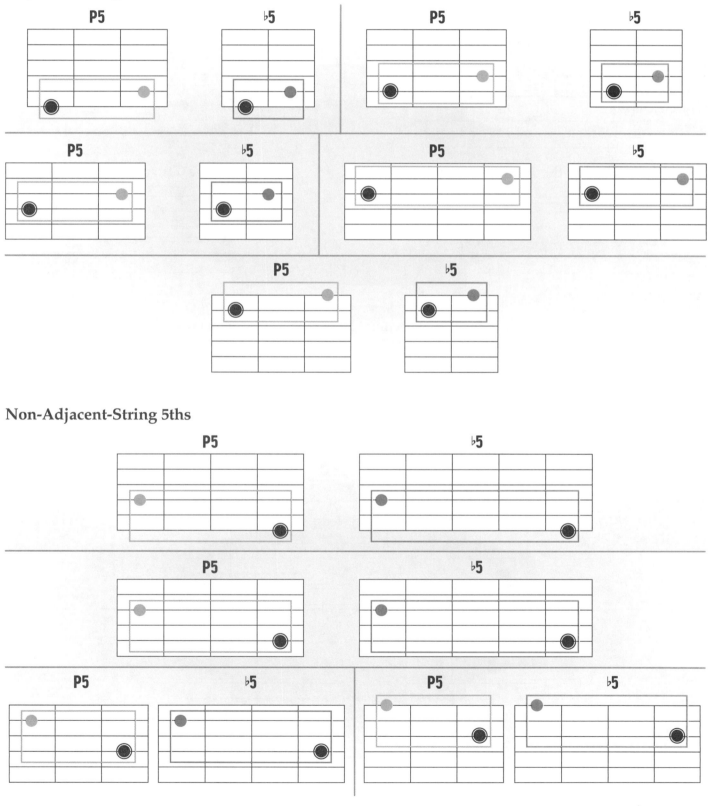

Non-Adjacent-String 5ths

The Diminished Triad

When we replace the natural 5th in a minor chord with a ♭5th, we get a *diminished* triad. Sometimes you'll see this represented by a "°" symbol, as in C°. Compare below:

Minor Triad:
Root–minor 3rd–5th

Diminished Triad:
Root–minor 3rd–♭5th

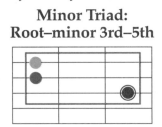 

Here's what the diminished triad looks like on all the string sets:

Root on the Sixth String

Root on the Fifth String

Root on the Fourth String

Root on the Third String

The ♯5th

The ♯5th interval is one half step *greater* than the natural 5th. Compare the following to see the difference between the perfect 5th (P5) and the ♯5th (♯5).

Adjacent-String 5ths

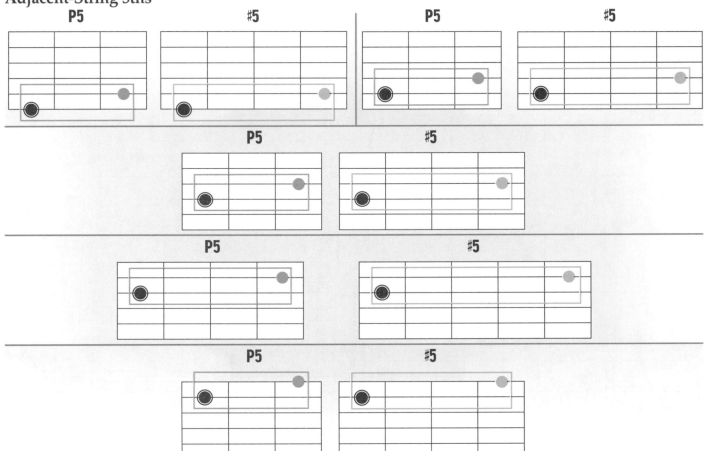

Non-Adjacent-String 5ths

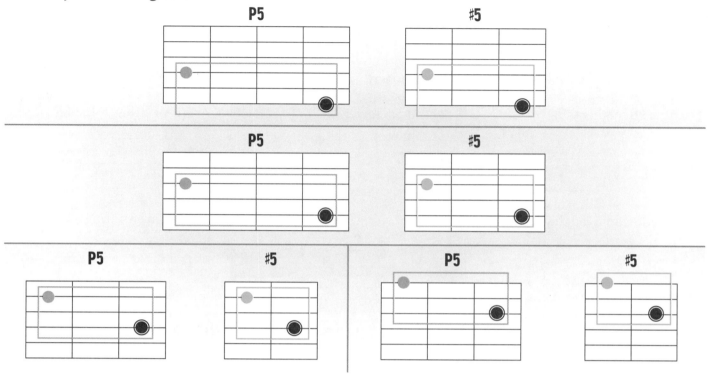

The Augmented Triad

When we replace the natural 5th in a major chord with a #5th, we get an *augmented* triad. The symbol for augmented is usually "+," as in C+. Compare below:

Major Triad:
Root–major 3rd–5th

Augmented Triad:
Root–major 3rd–#5th

Here's what the augmented triad looks like on all the string sets:

Root on the Sixth String

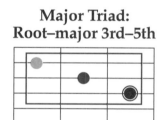

Root on the Fifth String

Root on the Fourth String

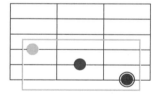

Root on the Third String

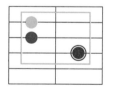

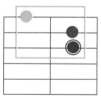

DIG DEEPER

We can also say the following about 5ths:

- A natural (or perfect) 5th spans seven half steps, or...
- A natural 5th spans three whole steps and one half step.
- A ♭5th (or diminished 5th) spans six half steps, or...

- A ♭5th spans three whole steps.
- A #5th (or augmented 5th) spans eight half steps, or...
- A #5th spans four whole steps.

CHAPTER 4 QUIZ

The answers to each chapter quiz can be found in the Appendix. The first example in each section below is done for you.

A. Add the Requested Note to the One Shown

1. Non-adjacent string, natural 5th higher.

2. Adjacent string, natural 5th lower.

3. Adjacent string, ♭5th higher.

4. Adjacent string, ♯5th higher.

5. Adjacent string, ♭5th lower.

6. Non-adjacent string, ♯5th lower.

B. Identify the Following Intervals as Perfect 5th (P5), ♭5th (♭5), or ♯5th (♯5)

1.

♯5

2.

3.

4.

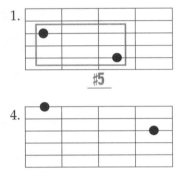

5.

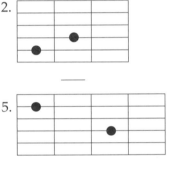

6.

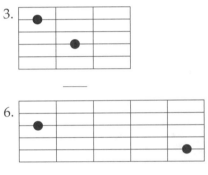

C. Identify the Following Triads as Diminished (dim) or Augmented (aug)

1.

dim

2.

3.

4.

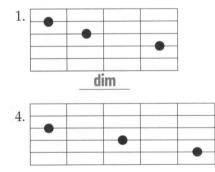

5.

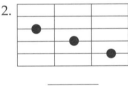
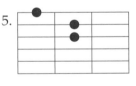

6.

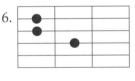
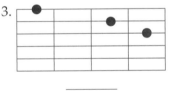

Chapter 4 Review

Before proceeding, make sure you have a good grip on the following:

- You know what perfect 5ths, ♭5ths, and ♯5ths look like on each adjacent string pair.
- You know what perfect 5ths, ♭5ths, and ♯5ths look like on each non-adjacent string pair.
- You understand that the 3rd is the determining factor in whether or not a chord is major or minor.
- You understand that the 5th (along with the 3rd) is the determining factor in whether the chord is diminished or augmented.
- You understand that a diminished triad contains a root, minor 3rd, and ♭5th.
- You understand that an augmented triad contains a root, major 3rd, and ♯5th.

CHAPTER 5
TRANSPOSING CHORD SHAPES

If you're up to speed on everything up to this point, this chapter shouldn't pose too much of a problem for you. What we're going to do is take those three-note triad voicings from the last chapter and *transpose* them to different roots, or keys. In other words, we might take a C major triad and transpose it to an E major triad.

We're still going to be dealing with all root-position chords here (i.e., the root will be the lowest-pitched note), but we're going to always move the shortest possible distance to the transposed chord. In other words, if it's shorter to move up or down a string set as opposed to up or down the neck (while staying on the same string set), then we'll do that. This will again test your knowledge of notes on the fretboard. Feel free to resort to the octave tricks shown in Chapter 1 if you need to.

We'll use a three-step process to do this:

1. Locate the new root note that's closest to where you are, on string 3 or lower.
2. Add the proper 5th.
3. Add the proper 3rd to complete the new triad.

Note that steps 2 and 3 can be reversed if it feels better to you. I prefer to add the 5th first because it prevents possibly having to re-fret the root and 3rd notes with different fingers.

DIG DEEPER

The word transpose can apply to just a few notes or an entire piece of music. It simply means to play the same thing but in a different key.

For example, if you take a major 3rd shape of C/E such as this: And move that up to a major 3rd shape of D/F♯, like this:

You've transposed that shape up a whole step (a distance of two frets). On the guitar, a capo is an easy way to do this!

Before we begin, take a second to look over the fretboard chart below and review the note names on strings 6 and 5. You can use this and the octave trick to quickly find the note name of any root on string 4 or string 3. In other words: What's the name of the note on fret 9 of string 4? Well, just play an octave below it, which is fret 7 of string 6. It's a B note!

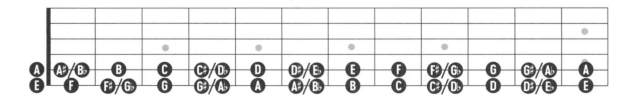

TRANSPOSING MAJOR AND MINOR TRIADS

OK, let's try our first transposition. We'll start with major triads. Let's move the following C major triad on strings 4–2 to an F major triad. (Remember: we can move up or down to the new chord. Our goal is to move the least amount of frets!)

C Major

Where's the closest F note to our root C note? It's just one string over, on string 3! So we add the new root:

Add the 5th to frame the shape:

And add the 3rd to complete the chord:

F Major

Let's try another one. We'll take this D minor triad on strings 3–1:

D Minor

Let's transpose it to a Bm chord. So, first, we need to find the closest B note to our root D note. Although there's one just three frets lower on string 3, there's one that's closer on string 4, just two frets away:

Now we add the 5th:

And we finish off the new chord by adding the minor 3rd:

B Minor

Let's try another major chord. We'll take this A major triad on strings 6–4:

A Major

And let's transpose it to G major. So, first, we find the G note that's on the fret closest to fret 5 (where our A root is located). Of course, there's one a whole step below, at fret 3 of string 6, but it turns out there's one closer than that! In fact, there's one on fret 5:

Now let's add the 5th to frame the shape:

Then add the major 3rd to complete the new chord:

G Major

Here's a trick to make sure you've found the closest new root note. Once you've found what you think is right, check the forward-facing octave shape to see if there's one closer. For instance, in the previous example, after finding the G note on fret 3, string 6 a whole step below A, you might think, "That's gotta be the closest one." But then if you check the forward-facing octave shape of G, you'd see the one at fret 5, string 4.

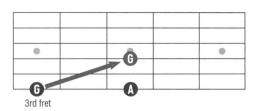

3rd fret

Finally, let's start with this G minor chord on strings 5–3:

G Minor

And we'll transpose it to an E minor chord. First, let's find the closest E that's on string 3 or lower. That would be this one on string 3, just one fret down:

Now let's add the 5th to frame the shape:

And we finish by adding the minor 3rd:

E Minor

TRANSPOSING DIMINISHED TRIADS

Let's try the same idea with a diminished triad. If you remember, a diminished triad contains a root, minor 3rd, and a ♭5th (also known as a *diminished 5th*). We'll start off with this B diminished chord on strings 3–1:

B°

Let's transpose this to a G diminished chord. First, let's find the closest G note. We actually have two possibilities that are equidistant: one on the fourth string and one on the sixth string. Both are one fret away from out root, B:

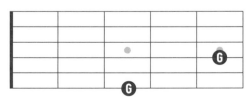

When we consider the chord shape, however, we can see that, by choosing the G on string 6, we'd have to move much farther (and this is besides the fact that playing a G diminished chord down there wouldn't be possible because we'd need a ♭5th note on string 4, which is unplayable). So we'll use the G note on string 4, fret 5. Next, we add the ♭5th to it:

And now we add the minor 3rd (also known as the ♭3rd) to finish the chord shape:

G°

TRANSPOSING AUGMENTED TRIADS

Finally, let's use the procedure on an augmented triad. As mentioned before, augmented triads aren't nearly as common as major or minor chords, but they do pop up from time to time. You can hear them prominently featured in "Real Love" (The Beatles), "Greatest Love of All" (Whitney Houston), and "Baby Hold On" (Eddie Money), to name just a few.

Let's start with a D augmented triad on strings 5–3:

D+

And let's transpose it to F+. First, we find the closest F note on string 3 or lower. That would be on string 4, here:

Now we add the ♯5th to frame the chord:

And, finally, we add the major 3rd to complete the chord:

F+

TRANSPOSING A SHAPE AND ALTERING THE CHORD TYPE

Now let's up the ante a bit. We'll not only transpose a triad shape, but we'll also change the triad type. To do this, we're going to start with the same three-step procedure we've been using. Then, once we have the transposed chord, we'll alter it to create the new quality. The same rules apply: we're going to use the same root/3rd/5th arrangement (low to high) and we want to move the least amount of frets.

Let's start with this C major triad on strings 4–2 again:

C Major

We want to change this to a D minor chord. Starting with our three-step procedure, we'll end up with this D major chord here:

D Major

Since we want a D minor chord, we just need to lower the 3rd a half step to make it a minor 3rd. So, we end up with this:

D Minor

Now let's try changing a minor chord into a diminished chord. We'll start with an Am chord on strings 4–2. (Notice that we're using the chord symbol "m" for a minor chord, which is widely used. You may also see "min" at times. They mean the same thing. A capital letter by itself, such as "C," implies a major chord.)

Am

Let's change it to F♯ diminished. After our three-step procedure, we end up with this F♯m chord:

F♯m

In order to change this to a diminished chord, we just need to lower the 5th a half step to a ♭5th:

F♯°

Let's do one more. We'll take this Em chord on strings 3–1:

Em

And we're going to change it to a D augmented chord. Our three-step procedure will get us this Dm chord on strings 6–4:

Dm

To make this a D augmented chord, we need to make two changes: we need to move the minor 3rd up a half step to a major 3rd, and we need to move the perfect 5th up a half step to a ♯5th. So, we'll end up with this:

D+

Notice that the shape of these chords (Em and D+) looks the same but, because of the guitar's tuning, they obviously sound very different!

CHAPTER 5 QUIZ

The answers to each chapter quiz can be found in the Appendix. The first example in each section below is done for you.

A. Transpose the Following Chords as Directed, with Minimal Fret Movement

1. Transpose to E♭ major:

B. Change Following Chords as Directed, with Minimal Fret Movement

1. Change to A major:

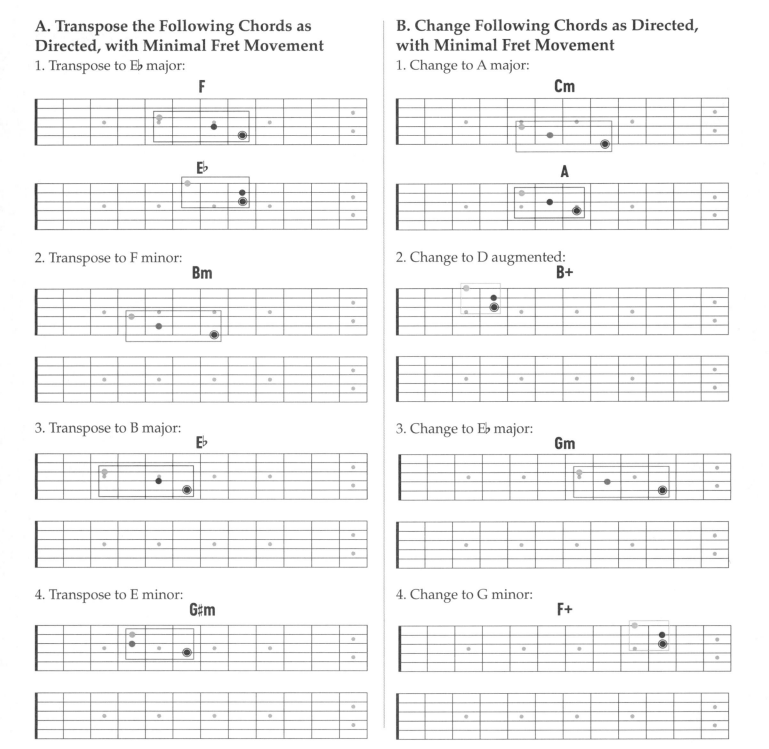

2. Transpose to F minor:

2. Change to D augmented:

3. Transpose to B major:

3. Change to E♭ major:

4. Transpose to E minor:

4. Change to G minor:

Chapter 5 Review

Before proceeding, make sure you have a good grip on the following:

- You know the note names on strings 6 and 5 and can use octaves to find the notes on the other strings.
- You know the note formulas for the four types of triads: **major:** root/major 3rd/5th, **minor:** root/minor 3rd/5th, **diminished:** root/minor 3rd/♭5th, **augmented:** root/major 3rd/♯5th.
- You're able to transpose a chord shape to another root without having to move a great distance on the fretboard.
- You're able to change a chord shape to a different root with a different chord quality without having to move a great distance on the fretboard.

CHAPTER 6
INVERSIONS

Up until this point, we've been dealing with chords and intervals in what's called root position, meaning that the root was always the lowest-pitched note. But that's not the only way to play a chord or interval. When a chord appears as an *inversion*, it simply means that a note other than the root of the chord is on bottom. That concept is what we're going to look at in this chapter. You may already make use of chord inversions all the time and not know it. After this chapter, however, you'll know the "why" and "how" behind them.

We'll start with inverted intervals. These are pretty easy to recognize on the guitar once you know all the octave shapes. By now, you should be getting pretty familiar with them. When we invert an interval, we simply flip the order of the notes. We can do this one of two ways: transfer the bottom note up an octave, or transfer the top note down an octave. Let's check it out…

INVERTING 5THS

Let's say we have the interval of C to G, a perfect 5th:

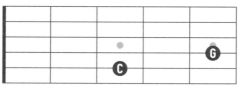

If we invert the interval, the notes will be G to C, from bottom to top. So, we can either bring the G down an octave, like this:

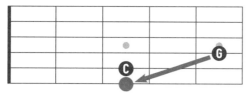

Or we can move the C note up an octave, like this:

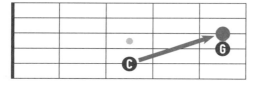

The result is the same, only they're displaced by an octave.

Same Dyad in Two Different Octaves

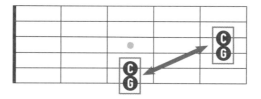

Note: Whereas a triad is a three-note chord, a *dyad* is just—you guessed it—a two-note chord.

The other difference is that we're left with a new interval—it's not a 5th anymore. This interval, from G up to C, is a *4th*. Specifically, it's a *perfect 4th*.

Interval "Quantity"

The numeric part of an interval (i.e., the 3rd in "major 3rd" or the 5th in "perfect 5th") is known as its *quantity*, and it's really a pretty simple concept. To find the quantity of an interval, you just count note names through the musical alphabet:

- What's C to D? Count the note names: C (1)–D (2). It's a 2nd.
- What's E to G? Count and find out: E (1)–F (2)–G (3). It's a 3rd.
- What's F to C? Count up (remember that the alphabet restarts after G): F (1)–G (2)–A (3)–B (4)–C (5). It's a 5th.

It gets more specific than that, as we've seen. For example, we can have a major 3rd or a minor 3rd. We can have a perfect 5th, a diminished 5th (♭5th), or an augmented 5th (♯5th), etc. This is the other half of the interval equation: the *quality*. And that's determined by the precise distance (i.e., the number of half steps) from the root of the other chord tones. But none of that changes the quantity; it's always verified by simply counting note names.

So, knowing what we now know about interval quantity, we can easily see why G to C is a 4th. Just count up: G (1)–A (2)–B (3)–C (4). And, more specifically, this is a perfect 4th.

Perfect 4ths

Let's look at the perfect 4th shape on each string group. These will all be adjacent string groups, as non-adjacent 4ths are a bit too stretchy to be practical.

DIG DEEPER

We can also say the following about 4ths:

- The 4th interval is located between the 3rd and 5th (seems self-evident enough, yes?)
- A perfect 4th spans five half steps, or…
- A perfect 4th spans two whole steps and one half step, or…
- A perfect 4th is one half step greater than a major 3rd.

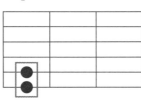
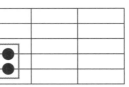

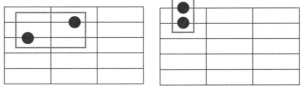

Other Types of 4ths

As a quick exercise, let's look at other types of 4ths. If we move one half step higher, we get a ♯*4th*, or *augmented 4th*, which spans three whole steps and looks like this on strings 6–5:

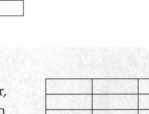

Do you recognize that shape? You're right! It's the same as the ♭5th (or diminished 5th). Musical context will determine whether we call it a ♭5th or a ♯4th.

What about a half step *below* a 4th? Is that a diminished 4th? That would be a really good guess, but it's actually incorrect. Take a look here to see why:

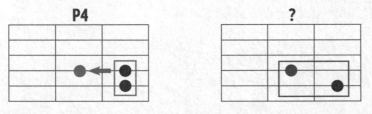

Surely you recognize that shape, right? Yes, it's a major 3rd! So that's why we only have two different types of 4ths: a perfect 4th and an augmented 4th (♯4th).

Let's look at another example. This time, we'll start with a 4th interval of C to F on strings 5–4:

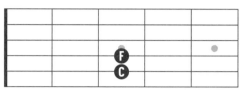

Again, to invert the interval, we either move the bottom note up an octave or the top note down an octave. So, we're left with these two possibilities:

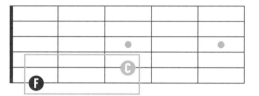

What do those look like? That's right—5ths! Do you see a pattern? This is inversion rule #1:

- 5ths always invert to 4ths, and…
- 4ths always invert to 5ths.

INVERTING 3RDS

Now let's look at our 3rd intervals. We can invert them the same way we did with 5ths: we move the bottom note up an octave or the top note down an octave. Let's start with the major 3rd interval of C to E on strings 5–4:

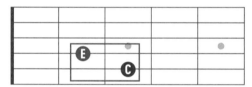

After moving the bottom note up, we get this shape:

And here's what we get when we move the top note down an octave:

Do you recognize this shape? If you said, "♯5th" (or "augmented 5th"), you're absolutely right. However, just as with the ♭5th, this interval goes by another name, as well. It's also called a *minor 6th*.

As you remember, these shapes can also be played on non-adjacent string pairs, like this (we've transposed the lower shape up an octave to make it feasible):

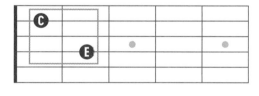

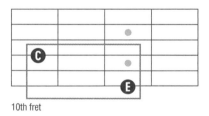

10th fret

Let's invert a minor 3rd interval now. We'll use this D to F interval on strings 5–4:

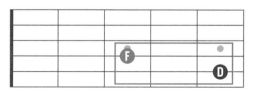

After moving the bottom note up or the top note down, we end up with these shapes:

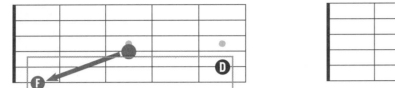

These are *major 6th* intervals, which are new to us. They can also be played with non-adjacent string pairs, as we'll soon see.

This brings us to inversion rule #2:
- *Major* 3rds invert to *minor* 6ths, and…
- *Minor* 3rds invert to *major* 6ths.

DIG DEEPER

Just as with the ♯4th/♭5th situation, the musical context determines whether we call it a minor 6th or a ♯5th. Remember our quantity rule in this regard: For it to be a 5th—*any* kind of 5th—it *must* contain five note names. A 6th—*any* kind of 6th—*must* contain six note names.

For example, let's say we have this interval:

The bottom note is a G, but what's the top note? It could be a D♯ or an E♭.

- If the note is called D♯, then the interval is an augmented 5th (♯5th) because there are only *five* note names involved:
  G (1)–A (2)–B (3)–C (4)–D♯ (5).

- If the note is called E♭, then the interval is a minor 6th (♭6th) because there are *six* note names involved:
  G (1)–A (2)–B (3)–C (4)–D (5)–E♭ (6).

Minor 6ths

Let's take a look at minor 6th shapes on adjacent and non-adjacent string pairs. Again, you'll recognize these because they look the same as the ♯5th shape. They also sound the same, so they are colored accordingly.

Adjacent String Pairs

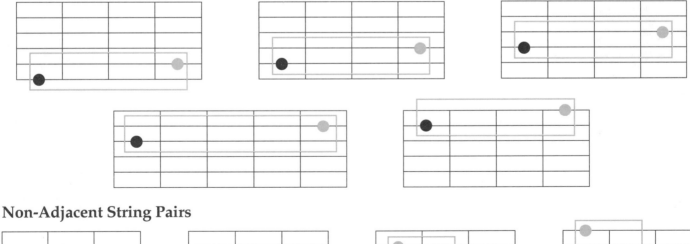

Non-Adjacent String Pairs

Major 6ths

Below, you'll find what the major 6ths look like on both adjacent and non-adjacent string pairs. Again, notice that the major 6ths are simply one half step larger than the minor 6ths, just as major 3rds are one half step larger than minor 3rds.

Adjacent String Pairs

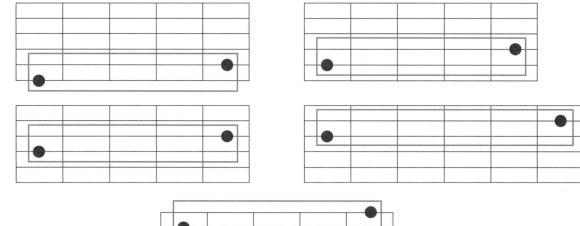

Non-Adjacent String Pairs

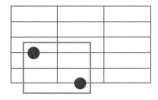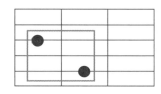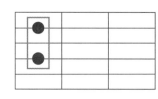

DIG DEEPER

We can also say the following about minor 6ths:
- A minor 6th spans eight half steps, or…
- A minor 6th spans four whole steps, or…
- A minor 6th is one half step greater than a perfect 5th.

And we can say the following about major 6ths:
- A major 6th spans nine half steps, or…
- A major 6th spans four whole steps and one half step, or…
- A major 6th is a whole step greater than a perfect 5th.

INVERTING TRIADS

This is where the fun starts. Armed with your new knowledge of inverted 5ths and 3rds, we can start applying those concepts to whole triads.

Although we're dealing with three notes instead of two, the inversion process is still the same: you either move the bottom note up an octave or move the top note down an octave. Let's check out the process with a C major triad on strings 6–4, which is arranged in root position (root–3rd–5th, low to high):

C

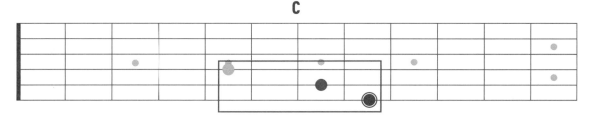

Let's start by moving the bottom note, C, up an octave. Since we want to play these as chords, we'll need to move it up to string 3 with a backward-facing octave shape. We'll end up with, from low to high, 3rd–5th–root.

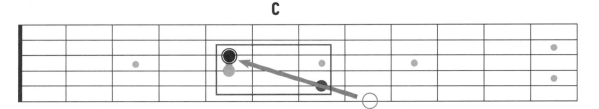

C

We can do this same process again, moving the bottom note (the 3rd, E) up an octave with a backward-facing shape. We'll end up with, from low to high, 5th–root–3rd:

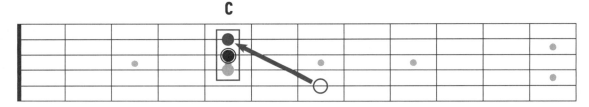

C

Now let's do the same thing again, moving the bottom note (the 5th, G) up an octave. We'll end up with, from low to high, root–3rd–5th. Note that this is exactly where we started, only an octave higher.

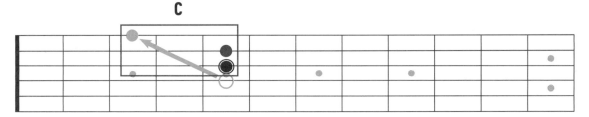

C

Also notice that our chord symbol, C, didn't change at all. These are all C chords; we've only rearranged the order in which the notes are stacked.

A Closer Examination

If you look closely, you can see our inverted intervals at work, as well. For example, if we look at our first chord (root position), we have a major 3rd interval and a perfect 5th interval:

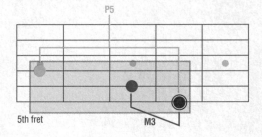

When we performed our first inversion, look what happens to those intervals:

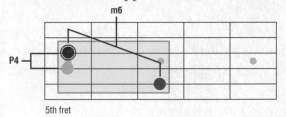

The major 3rd was inverted to a minor 6th, and the perfect 5th was inverted to a perfect 4th—just like our rules say!

Root Position

We don't need to spend much time talking about root position at all because we've been playing nothing but root-position triads up until this chapter. Root position simply means that the root is on the bottom of the chord. So, in a close-voiced chord—one in which all of the notes are within one octave (which we've been playing exclusively thus far)—the notes will be in the order of, low to high, root–3rd–5th.

Again, our C major chord from before was played in root position:

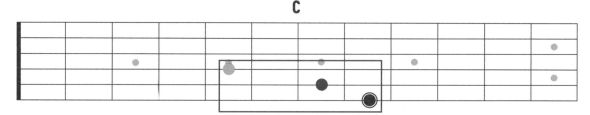

First Inversion

A chord is said to be in *first inversion* when its 3rd is on bottom. This means the notes will be arranged, low to high, 3rd–5th–root. This is the chord that results when you transfer the root of a triad up an octave. So, staying within the same area on the neck, our C major chord from above would look like this in first inversion:

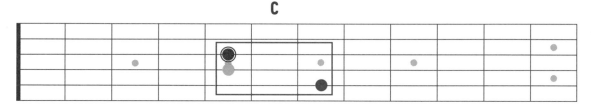

Jimi Hendrix would famously use this chord form in many of his songs, as have countless other players.

Second Inversion

A chord is in *second inversion* when its 5th is on bottom. This means the notes will be arranged, low to high, 5th–root–3rd. This is the result of continuing the process by moving the bottom note of a first-inversion chord up an octave. So, again remaining in the same neck position, our C major chord from above would look like this in second inversion:

This is a very useful shape because it can be barred with one finger, making it possible to easily add decorations with your other fingers.

These are the only three possibilities for a triad: root position, first inversion, and second inversion. Again, by continuing the bottom-note-up-an-octave process one more time, we end up where we started, only an octave higher.

The Big Picture

Keep in mind that these terms are only applying to the guitar as if it were a solo instrument. In actual practice with a full band, the guitarist could be playing the same chord over and over, while the bass could move from the root of the chord to the 3rd. This would create an overall first-inversion sound, even if the guitar player were still playing a root-position chord. Just listen to Paul McCartney's lines in the Beatles for an excellent example of a bassist implying inversions.

Nevertheless, guitar chords sound different when played in different inversions, so it's not only good practice to learn them for the benefit of understanding the neck; it's also very useful because they'll expand your tonal palette.

TRIAD INVERSION SHAPES

Just as we can play intervals on different string sets, we can do the same with triad inversions. We're going to take a look at them now. We'll use the same method as we did for the intervals, starting with the lowest string set and working upwards through each. The same color system will be in place to help you keep track of chord tones. In case you haven't learned it by heart yet, here's the color system for the chord degrees:

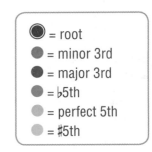

- ● = root
- ● = minor 3rd
- ● = major 3rd
- ● = ♭5th
- ● = perfect 5th
- ● = ♯5th

Major

Root Position

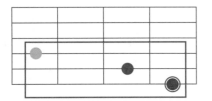

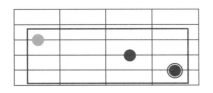

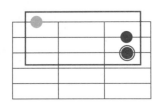

First Inversion

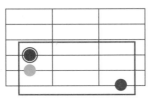

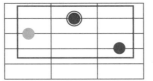

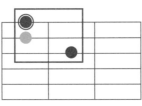

Second Inversion

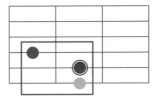

Keep Your Eye on the Root

When you're playing these shapes, always make sure you know where the root is located. The root can function as your anchor, allowing you to move these shapes at will, and at lightning speed. The goal is to be able to pick any note on the neck, think of it as a root, and then build a triad around it, whether it's the lowest note, middle note, or highest note in the voicing. By working through all these inversions and internalizing where the root is located in each, you'll eventually be able to do just that!

Minor

Root Position

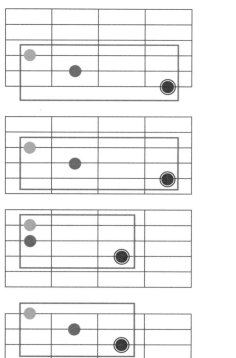

First Inversion

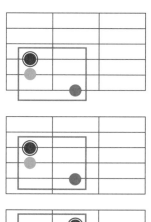

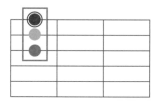

Second Inversion

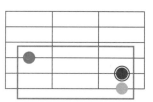

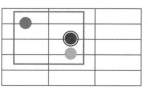
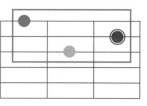

Also be sure to notice what changes between each chord quality. In other words, compare the first-inversion major shape with the first-inversion minor shapes to see how the 3rd has been lowered by a half step in the minor chord.

Diminished

Root Position

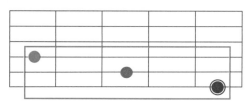

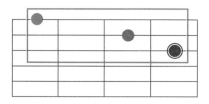

First Inversion

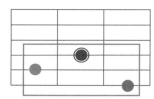
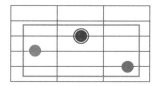
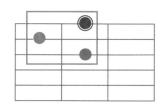

Second Inversion

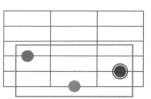
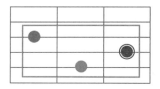

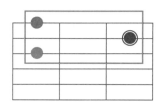

Augmented

Root Position   **First Inversion**   **Second Inversion**

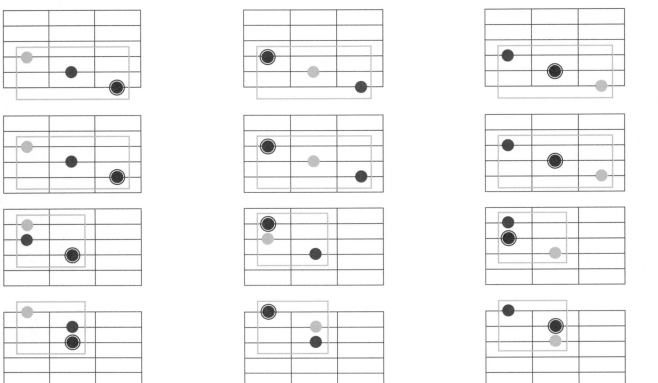

Did you notice anything interesting about those augmented voicings? That's right! The root-position, first-inversion, and second-inversion shapes all look exactly the same. It sure makes learning them easier! But be sure to keep your eye on the root so you know where it is.

DIG DEEPER

So, why do all the augmented inversions look the same? Well, the augmented chord is what's known as a *symmetrical* chord. This means that all the notes are equidistant from each other. In this case, they're all a major 3rd (four half steps, or two whole steps) apart. Take a C+ chord, for example:

- From the root (C) to the 3rd (E) is a major 3rd, or four half steps.
- From the 3rd (E) to the ♯5th (G♯) is also a major 3rd, or four half steps.
- And from the ♯5th (G♯) to the root (C) is… a major 3rd? Well, it's four half steps for sure. But isn't a 3rd supposed to involve only three note names? Yes, you're right! Great catch.

This is another interesting thing about the augmented chord: It seems to contradict itself when you try to spell it. In fact, if you respell the G♯ note as an A♭, then you do get a proper major 3rd up to the root. But, of course, by doing that, you mess up the major 3rd from E to G♯—ad infinitum.

Suffice it to say, an augmented chord is built with three notes that are all four half steps apart. There's no contradiction there! As we've seen, the benefit to this is that each "inversion" looks the same as the previous one. In essence, there are really only four different augmented chords because each one acts the same as two others.

- C+ contains the same notes as E+ and G♯+/A♭+.
- C♯+/D♭+ contains the same notes as F+ and A+.
- D+ contains the same notes as F♯+/G♭+ and A♯+/B♭+.
- D♯+/E♭+ contains the same notes as G+ and B+.

Talk about bang for your buck!

CHAPTER 6 QUIZ

The answers to each chapter quiz can be found in the Appendix. The first example in each section below is done for you.

A. Invert the Following Intervals by Moving the Bottom Note Up an Octave

Note: There are two possibilities for the new interval shape. Choose the one resulting in the voicing that spans the least amount of frets. In other words, choose the easiest-to-play voicing.

1.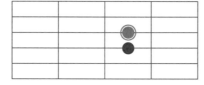

2.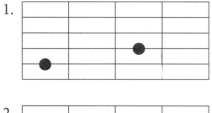

3.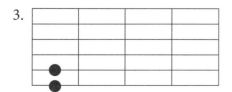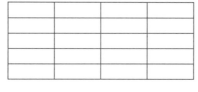

4.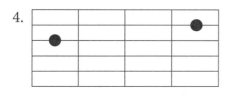

5.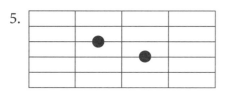

6.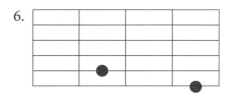

7.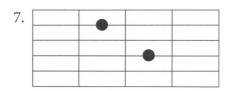

8.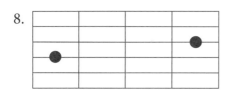

B. Identify the Following Intervals

(P = perfect, M = major, m = minor, d = diminished, a = augmented)

Some examples will have two possible answers.

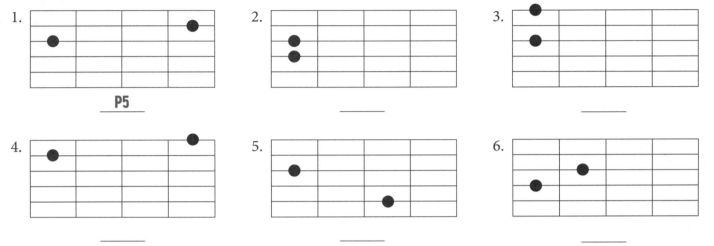

1. _**P5**_

2. _____

3. _____

4. _____

5. _____

6. _____

C. Identify the Following Triads

List their quality as major, minor, augmented, or diminished and their inversion as root pos., 1st inv., or 2nd inv.

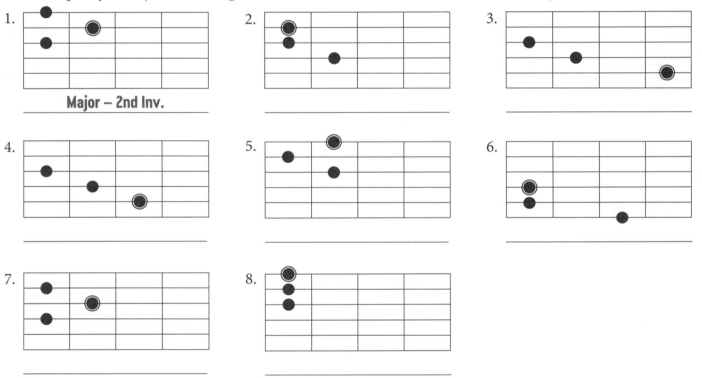

1. _**Major – 2nd Inv.**_

2. _____

3. _____

4. _____

5. _____

6. _____

7. _____

8. _____

Chapter 6 Review

Before proceeding, make sure you have a good grip on the following:

- You know how to invert an interval.
- A 5th interval always inverts to a 4th, and vice versa.
- A 3rd interval always inverts to a 6th interval, and vice versa (major 3rd to minor 6th, and minor 3rd to major 6th).
- You know the three possible inversions for triads: root position, first inversion, and second inversion.
- Root position = root on bottom, first inversion = 3rd on bottom, and second inversion = 5th on bottom.

CHAPTER 7
BUILDING SCALES

We now come to the point where we're just about ready to use our accumulated knowledge to start building scales. Before we do, though, let's quickly review what you know so far:

1. You're familiar with the following intervals:
   - **Half step** and **whole step**
   - **Minor 3rd** = three half steps
   - **Major 3rd** = four half steps
   - **Perfect 4th** = five half steps
   - **♯4th (or augmented 4th)** = six half steps
   - **♭5th (or diminished 5th)** = six half steps
   - **Perfect 5th** = seven half steps
   - **♯5th (or augmented 5th)** = eight half steps
   - **Minor 6th** = eight half steps
   - **Major 6th** = nine half steps
   - **Octave** = 12 half steps

2. You're familiar with the following triad types:
   - **Major:** root–3rd–5th
   - **Minor:** root–♭3rd–5th
   - **Diminished:** root–♭3rd–♭5th
   - **Augmented:** root–3rd–♯5th

3. You're familiar with the following triad inversions:
   - **Root position:** root on bottom
   - **First inversion:** 3rd on bottom
   - **Second inversion:** 5th on bottom

4. You know how to transpose chord and interval shapes to other positions and/or other string sets.

If any of these items are still a bit unclear, you may want to go back and review them in the earlier chapters before moving on. Once you're up to speed, let's move on!

FILLING IN THE GAPS

In a traditional major or minor scale, there are seven different notes in each octave (the eighth note would simply be the first note in a new octave). Looking at the list above, we can see that we've almost covered everything within the octave. We have 3rds, 4ths, 5ths, 6ths, and the octave. The only two intervals left are 2nds and 7ths, right? Well, that's not *entirely* true. Read on!

2ND INTERVALS

It turns out that you know even more than you realize you do, because half steps and whole steps go by other names, as well. They're the same as minor 2nds and major 2nds, respectively. In other words, a minor 2nd is one half step, such as from C to D♭:

Minor 2nd

And a major 2nd is two half steps, or one whole step, such as C to D:

Major 2nd

So, you already know all the fingerings for these 2nd intervals. If you need brushing up on them, just go back to Chapter 2 and substitute "minor 2nd" for "half step" and substitute "major 2nd" for "whole step."

7TH INTERVALS

The 7th is our final stop en route to the octave, which takes us back to where we started. As with 2nds, 3rds, and 6ths, there are two different kinds of 7th intervals: major 7th and minor 7th. Again, the minor version is one half step smaller than the major version. Let's see how they look on the fretboard.

Major 7ths

Major 7th intervals are normally played as a forward-facing non-adjacent pair (skipping one string). However, they do get played as a backward-facing pair (skipping two strings) at times, as well, especially on the higher strings. So, we'll look at both options.

Forward-Facing Major 7ths

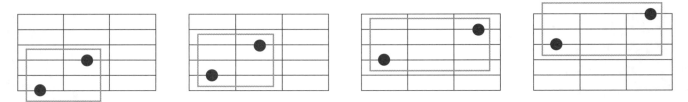

Backward-Facing Major 7ths

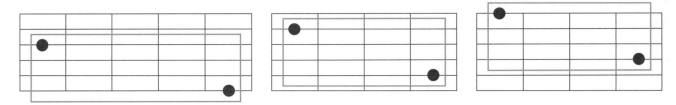

So Close!
Be sure to notice how close these major 7th shapes are to the octave shapes. They're only one half step smaller! This will come into play a bit more when we look at scales. For now, just register the fact that the major 7th interval is the largest interval we have before reaching the octave.

Minor 7ths

One half step smaller than a major 7th, minor 7ths are usually played as a non-adjacent pair (skipping one string). However, occasionally—especially in blues boogie rhythm patterns—they are played as adjacent-string pairs. It's an awfully big stretch on the lower frets! But we'll look at both types.

Adjacent-String Minor 7ths

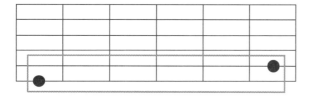
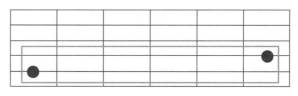

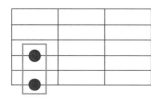

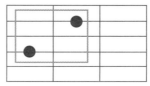
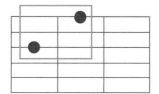

Forward-Facing Minor 7ths

DIG DEEPER

We can also say the following about minor 7ths:
- A minor 7th spans 10 half steps, or…
- A minor 7th spans five whole steps, or…
- A minor 7th is one whole step below an octave.

And we can say the following about major 7ths:
- A major 7th spans 11 half steps, or…
- A major 7th spans five whole steps and one half step, or…
- A major 7th is one half step below an octave.
- A major 7th is the largest interval within an octave.

MORE INVERSIONS

So, we've got:

- 5ths inverting to 4ths, and vice versa.
- 6ths inverting to 3rds, and vice versa.

Do you think there might be a connection between 7ths and 2nds? Absolutely! Inverted, 7ths become 2nds, and vice versa. And just as with 3rds/6ths, the quality flips when you invert the interval. In other words:

- A *major* 7th inverts to a *minor* 2nd.
- A *minor* 7th inverts to a *major* 2nd.

Check it out:

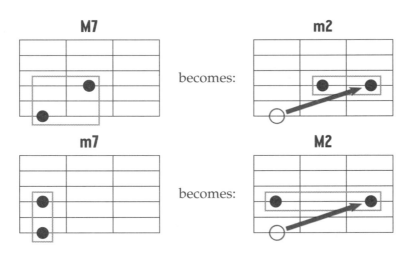

And the other way, with harmonic 2nds (dyads) inverting to 7ths, looks like this:

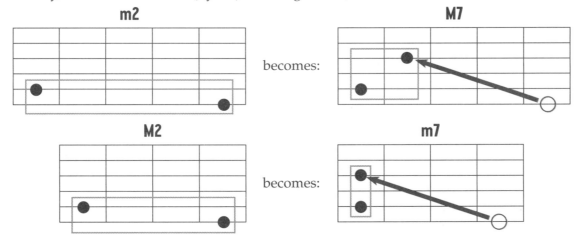

BUILDING A MAJOR SCALE

A major scale, as previously mentioned, contains seven different notes. And guess what… you already know the intervals for each one of those notes! Every scale starts with a root, which is also called the *tonic*. From there, it's fleshed out with one of each interval (one type of 2nd, one type of 3rd, etc.).

For a major scale—the "happy" scale—it's pretty darn easy. We simply use the major and perfect versions of all the intervals. Therefore, a major scale will contain:

Tonic   Major 2nd   Major 3rd   Perfect 4th   Perfect 5th   Major 6th   Major 7th

We finish it off with an octave on top, which can also be seen as the beginning of the scale in the next octave. Let's check it out with the C major scale. You should easily recognize each one of these shapes by now. Notice that our triad chord tones are still color-coded as before.

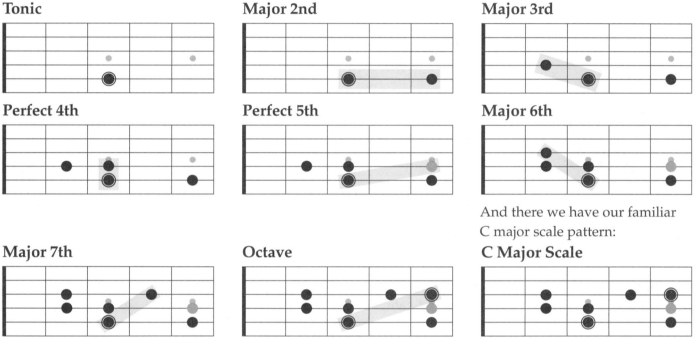

And there we have our familiar C major scale pattern:

Major Scale Formula

There's a well-known major scale "formula" that you may have heard before, and it goes like this:

Whole Step – Whole Step – Half Step – Whole Step – Whole Step – Whole Step – Half Step

This is usually abbreviated as simply, "Whole, whole, half, whole, whole, whole, half." What does this mean? Well, it's simply telling you the distance between each note of the scale. In other words, first you move a whole step from the tonic to the 2nd. Then you move another whole step from the 2nd to the 3rd. Then you move a half step from the 3rd to the 4th, and so on. We can see this play out in our scale form from above:

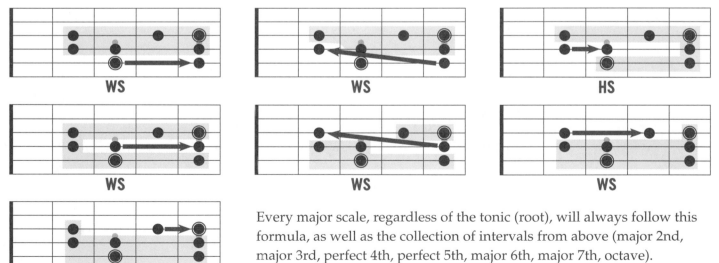

Every major scale, regardless of the tonic (root), will always follow this formula, as well as the collection of intervals from above (major 2nd, major 3rd, perfect 4th, perfect 5th, major 6th, major 7th, octave).

BUILDING A MINOR SCALE

The minor scale is the depressed sibling of the major scale. It had a lot in common at one point, but somewhere along the line, it turned to the dark side. It has seven different notes, as well, and shares many intervals with the major scale. In fact, there are only three notes that are different.

It would perhaps be most intuitive to think that, since the major scale contained the *major* versions of the 2nd, 3rd, 6th, and 7th intervals, the minor scale should contain the *minor* versions of those. Close, but no cigar. Although the minor scale does contain a minor 3rd, minor 6th, and minor 7th, it also contains a *major* 2nd. So, altogether, it looks like this:

Tonic   Major 2nd   Minor 3rd   Perfect 4th   Perfect 5th   Minor 6th   Minor 7th

So, if we start with our C major scale, we can simply lower the 3rd, 6th, and 7th by a half step:

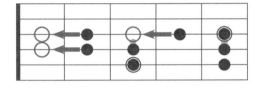

And we'll end up with the C minor scale:

C Minor Scale

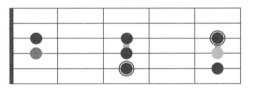

Granted, this may not be the most commonly played minor scale fingering, but it was used to show how it relates to the major scale. To make it more fret-hand friendly, we can just move the ♭3rd and ♭6th down a string set, like this:

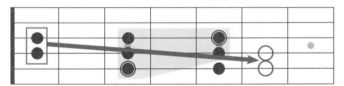

And we end up with this more common minor scale shape:

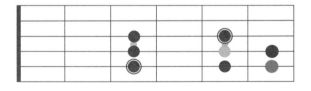

Minor Scale Formula

Just as the major scale can be expressed as "whole, whole, half, whole, whole, whole, half," the minor scale can be expressed with its own formula of whole and half steps. It looks like this:

Whole Step – Half Step – Whole Step – Whole Step – Half Step – Whole Step – Whole Step

This formula is not nearly as common as the major one. I think this is most likely because people usually find it easier and/or more helpful to simply compare the minor scale to the major scale.

CHAPTER 7 QUIZ

The answers to each chapter quiz can be found in the Appendix. The first example in the first two sections below is done for you.

A. Identify the Following Intervals as Major 7th (M7) or Minor 7th (m7)

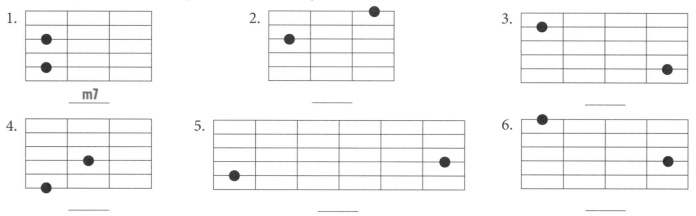

B. Circle the Appropriate Note in the Following Scale Shapes

Note: The tonic note is already circled in each.

1. Circle the **6th**:   2. Circle the **4th**:   3. Circle the **2nd**:   4. Circle the ♭**7th**:

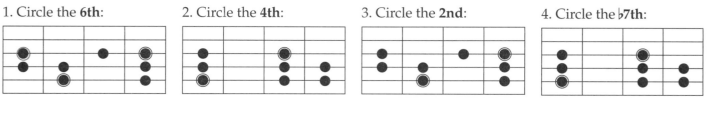

C. Fill in the Blanks in the Following Scale Formulas

1. **Major Scale:** whole – whole – half – whole – ? – whole – half

   _____

2. **Minor Scale:** tonic – major 2nd – minor 3rd – ? – perfect 5th – minor 6th – minor 7th

   _____

3. **Minor Scale:** whole – half – whole – whole – half – ? – whole

   _____

4. **Major Scale:** root – major 2nd – major 3rd – perfect 4th – perfect 5th – major 6th – ?

   _____

Chapter 7 Review

Before proceeding, make sure you have a good grip on the following:

- You know what minor and major 7th intervals look like on various string pairs.
- A major 7th interval inverts to a minor 2nd.
- A minor 7th interval inverts to a major 2nd.
- A major scale contains seven different tones: tonic – major 2nd – major 3rd – perfect 4th – perfect 5th – major 6th – major 7th.
- A major scale's formula is: whole – whole – half – whole – whole – whole – half
- A minor scale contains seven different tones: tonic – major 2nd – minor 3rd – perfect 4th – perfect 5th – minor 6th – minor 7th.
- A minor scale's formula is: whole – half – whole – whole – half – whole – whole

CHAPTER 8
TRANSPOSING SCALE SHAPES

This chapter is similar to Chapter 5, but we'll be using scale shapes instead of chords. Many of the same concepts will apply, though, so it shouldn't pose too much of a problem for you. We'll start simply and progress from there.

MOVING MAJOR SCALE SHAPES

We're going to start with one-octave scale shapes and work on moving them to different octaves. Let's begin with our C major scale shape from the previous chapter:

Forward-Facing Octave Transposition

Perhaps the easiest approach here is to move this shape up an octave with forward-facing octave shapes. In other words, you simply take the notes on each string and move them up with the forward-facing octave shape from Chapter 1:

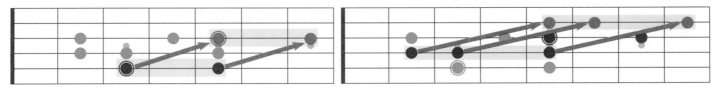

So our transposed shape looks like this:

C Major Scale

Notice how you can still recognize the intervals of the triad chord tones in the new shape. They look different now, of course, because of the B string transition, but you should know these interval shapes well by now.

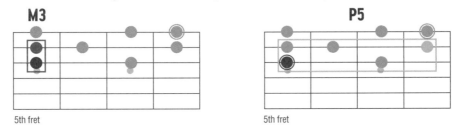

Backward-Facing Octave Transposition

We can take this new shape and transfer it down an octave by using a backward-facing octave shape.

We use the same process, transposing the shape one string at a time:

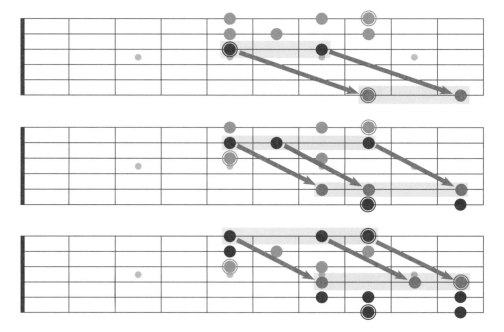

And so our new shape looks like this:

C Major Scale

Notice that, because the B string is not traversed in this shape, the scale looks identical to our original one based off the fifth string; it's just moved up five frets and down one string.

Important!

Remember that my terms "forward-facing" and "backward-facing" are named with respect to the *lower*-pitched note. In other words, even if you move *down* an octave like this:

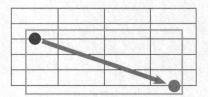

It's still a *forward-facing* octave shape because the lowest-pitched note is on the *lower* fret. By the same token, if we move a note down an octave like this:

It's still a *backward-facing* octave shape because the lowest-pitched note is on the *higher* fret. So just remember to think of these labels from the lower pitch's point of view.

Shampoo, Rinse, Repeat

We can continue this process—moving the shape up an octave with a forward-facing (FF) shape and down an octave with a backward-facing (BF) shape—until we're back where we started. Once we do that, the neck will look like this:

C Major Scale

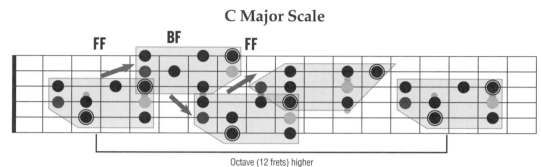

Octave (12 frets) higher

You can see that we've covered an entire octave by doing nothing but transposing one-octave shapes around. Granted, there are some holes left in certain areas, and we'll address those in a bit, but the idea is that the neck isn't this tangled web that it may seem at first. It's simply a collection of recognizable shapes that repeat throughout.

MOVING MINOR SCALE SHAPES

The process is the same for the minor scale. Let's start with our C minor scale in third position:

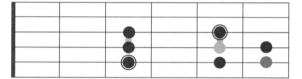

We can first move it up an octave with the forward-facing octave shape, the same way we did with the major scale. Since the process is the same, we won't go through it string by string again, but you can certainly do that if you find it helpful. We'll end up with this:

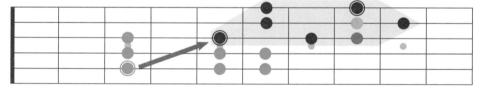

Continuing on, we move that shape down an octave with a backward-facing octave shape:

Again, notice how this shape looks identical to our original one based off the fifth string because the B string was not involved.

When we continue on, we end up where we started, only an octave higher:

C Minor Scale

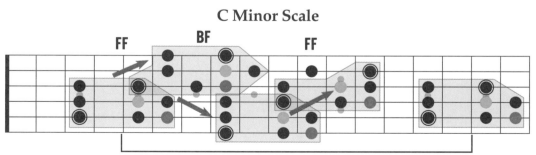

Octave (12 frets) higher

Patterns, Patterns, Patterns!

Don't fail to notice all the patterns here that repeat over and over. For example, even though the overall scale shape may look different on the higher strings because of the B string, it's important to notice that the shape still contains a repeating three-string pattern. The bottom string of each shape contains one whole step and one half step. The middle string of each shape contains the same. And the top string contains one whole step.

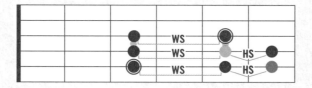

This holds true no matter what the overall shape looks like. Another pattern is the set of parallel perfect 4ths created on the bottom two strings of the shape. We'll use a different octave shape here to demonstrate but, again, this set of perfect 4ths happens in every one of these one-octave minor scale shapes.

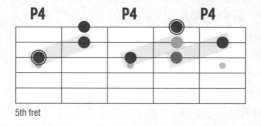

The more patterns like these you can recognize, the better you'll be able to "connect the dots" in your mind.

FILLING IN THE GAPS

As we've seen previously, even after moving our one-octave scale shapes around to cover one octave on the neck, there are still some gaps in places. While you could easily look online and find full-neck diagrams for the C major scale (or just about any other scale), the aim of this book is to help you see the connections and patterns that help make sense of this web of notes. To this end, it's helpful to fill in the gaps yourself by simply using the same octave tricks.

How is this done? It's pretty simple really. You simply find a gap on the neck and then look to the closest scale shape immediately in front of it (higher frets) or behind it (lower frets). Then you use either forward-facing or backward-facing octave shapes to fill in the gap.

Let's give it a try with our C major scale. Let's say we want to fill in this gap here:

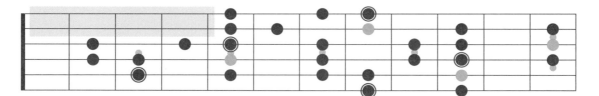

Well, we don't have a shape behind it because the nut is there, so we look to the shape directly in front of it and start filling in the gaps with backward-facing octaves. Just go string by string, ignoring any notes that you don't need. The closest shape directly in front of our gap would be this one here:

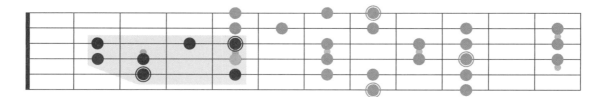

So, we just need to start from the bottom string of the shape and use a backward-facing octave shape to transpose the notes up an octave. First, we'll do string 5:

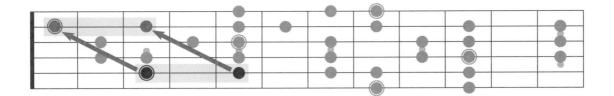

Then we move on to string 4 and do the same thing:

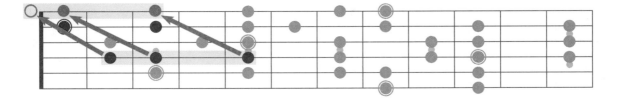

And there you have it; the gap is filled in. You can fill in the entire neck using this same procedure anywhere there's a gap. This works for any major/minor scale in any key.

As I said, it's easy enough to just find a scale chart online and memorize it by rote. But, in my opinion, you'll learn much more and understand the patterns much better if you work through the neck with this method, so I highly recommend it. I should mention that the same procedure will work for any scale—major, minor, or otherwise.

CHAPTER 8 QUIZ

The answers to each chapter quiz can be found in the Appendix. The first example in the first section below is done for you.

A. Transpose the Following Scale Shapes as Directed

1. Use a forward-facing octave shape to transpose up an octave:

D Major

2. Use a backward-facing octave shape to transpose up an octave:

B Minor

3. Use a forward-facing octave shape to transpose down an octave:

A Major

4. Use a backward-facing octave shape to transpose down an octave:

C# Minor

B. Fill in the Indicated Gap in the Scale Diagram

1. C Major Scale

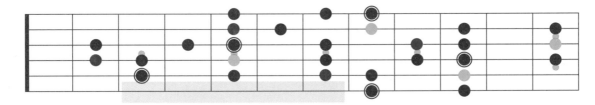

2. G Major Scale

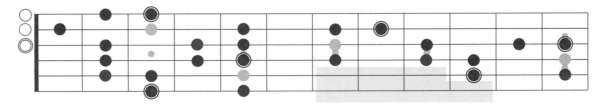

3. D Minor Scale

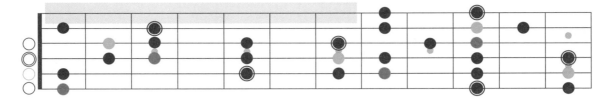

Chapter 8 Review

Before proceeding, make sure you have a good grip on the following:

- You know how to use forward- or backward-facing octave shapes to transpose a scale shape up or down an octave.
- You're able to "fill in the gaps" in any scale diagram by octave-transposing notes from a nearby scale form.

CHAPTER 9
CHORD PROGRESSION ROOT PATTERNS

This final chapter will be kind of a fun one—a little reward for all your hard work thus far. What we're going to do here is look at the patterns that are created by the root notes of chords in some common chord progressions to see what they look like on the fretboard. This can help you make some sense of these progressions with regard to how they tie in with the key and its matching major or minor scale.

PARAMETERS

We're going to work within a set of parameters here so as not to spread ourselves too thin.

Chords and Chord Type

- We'll only be using major and minor chords.
- We'll only be using E Form and A Form chords in open or barred form.

Just to review, and to make sure we're on the same page, let's clarify that last point. This is an open E chord:

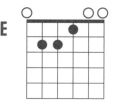

And this is an E-Form G barre chord in major and minor forms:

This is an open A chord:

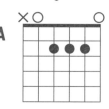

And this is an A-Form C barre chord in major (two possibilities) and minor form:

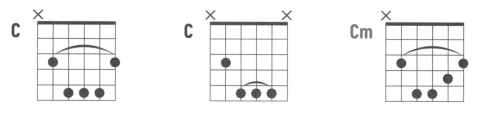

So, whenever you see a root note on the fretboard, that symbolizes either an E Form (if it's on string 6) or an A Form (if it's on string 5) chord.

Color System

We're going to be retaining certain elements of our previous color-coding system here: major chords will be identified with a red root and minor chords will be shown with a blue root. This, of course, is similar to our using red for a major 3rd interval and major triad and blue for a minor 3rd interval and minor triad. Also, the tonic of the key will be circled each time it appears.

So, for example, in the following:

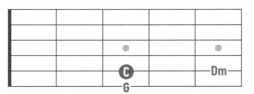

We have a C major chord, a D minor chord, and a G major chord, and we're in the key of C (i.e., C is the tonic).

A Quick Review

As mentioned earlier in the book, the words *root* and *tonic* are often used interchangeably. However, *root* is most often applied to a chord—the "root" is the note after which the chord is named—while *tonic* is most often applied to scales. In a C major scale, for example, the note C is the *tonic*, D is the 2nd, E is the 3rd, etc. In a C chord, however, C is the *root*, E is the 3rd, etc. *Tonic* is also generally applied when talking about the key of a song. If you have a song in E major, for example, E is the *tonic*.

One distinction that's generally upheld is that *tonic* applies to the same note within a key. In the key of C, for example, the note C is always the *tonic*. The term *root*, though, can be applied to other notes within the key when talking about chords. For example, you could be in the key of C but be talking about an F chord. In that case, F would be the *root* of the chord, but C would still be the *tonic* of the key.

Roman Numerals

Roman numerals are typically used to identify chords within a key. As you know, there are seven different notes in a major scale, and each one of those notes can be the root of a chord. As shorthand, Roman numerals are assigned to these chords: uppercase for major chords and lowercase for minor chords. Take the key of C, for example. If we write out its notes, it looks like this:

Tonic	2nd	3rd	4th	5th	6th	7th
C	D	E	F	G	A	B

Represented in Roman numerals, it looks like this:

I	ii	iii	IV	V	vi	vii°
C	Dm	Em	F	G	Am	B°

Note that we have:
- Three major chords: I (C), IV (F), and V (G)
- Three minor chords: ii (Dm), iii (Em), and vi (Am)
- And one diminished chord: vii° (B°)

This pattern of chord types holds true in any major key. Similar to the W–W–H–W–W–W–H formula for the scale, the formula for the chords of any major key is:

major – minor – minor – major – major – minor – diminished

Note: The diminished chord is not very common, and we won't be using it in any of our progressions.

MAJOR-KEY PROGRESSIONS

Let's start with some progressions in major keys. Some of these have literally been used in thousands of songs and will likely appear in thousands more. It really is quite amazing how they can still be used to generate unique-sounding material.

You should recognize many of the patterns here from the scale forms you've seen. For simplicity, we'll demonstrate all of these in the key of C major, but these patterns can be transposed to any key simply by sliding them to the appropriate location. Two patterns will be shown for each progression.

I–IV–V

Probably the most common chord progression of all time, the I–IV–V is timeless. Here it is in the key of C:

Hint: Do you recognize the inverted intervals here? Take a look at what happened to the F and G notes in the second diagram and then take a quick peek back at Chapter 6.

ii–V–I

This is a staple of jazz, but it can be heard in a lot of older blues and pop tunes, as well.

I–vi–ii–V

This is kind of an expanded version of the ii–V–I and is known as a *turnaround* progression.

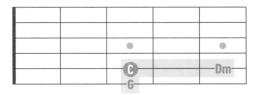

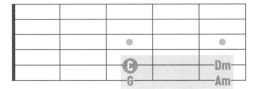

I–V–vi–IV

This one is probably the most common progression of the past 30 years. It, and its various manifestations (e.g., beginning on the vi chord and playing vi–IV–I–V) has been used in so many songs that it's had parody videos made about it on YouTube. Check out "Four Chord Song" by Axis of Awesome to hear what I mean.

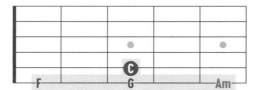

I–ii–iii–IV

Just walk it on up! You can hear this idea in lots of songs, as well. Often, it will even continue on to the V chord, as it does in Bob Dylan's "Like a Rolling Stone."

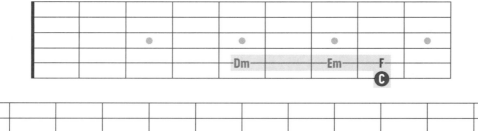

DIG DEEPER

The term *relative minor* describes the relationship between the keys of A minor and C major. Relative major and minor keys share all the same notes, but they just consider different notes the tonic. Both C major and A minor, for example, contain the notes C–D–E–F–G–A–B, but in C major, the note C is the tonic (or "home"); in A minor, A is the tonic.

The *Cliff Notes* version might read something like this: Songs in the keys of A minor and C major might use mostly the same chords, but the song in A minor will likely end on an A minor chord, while the song in C major would likely end on a C major chord. Granted, it's not as simple as all that, and there are exceptions for sure, but that's a good start in any case.

MINOR-KEY PROGRESSIONS

There are lots of staple minor-key progressions, as well. So let's take a look at them. For simplicity, we'll look at all of these in the key of A minor. (A minor is the *relative minor* of C major. See sidebar for more details.)

♭VI–♭VII–i

This is a classic minor-key progression that's equally at home in a metal song or an acoustic ballad.

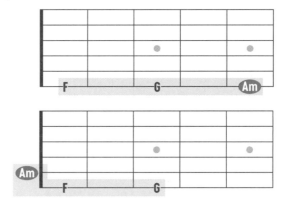

i–♭VII–♭VI–V

This one is bending the rules just a tad, because the v chord in a minor key is technically supposed to be minor. But it's so common to make it major in a minor key that it's almost more the rule than the exception.

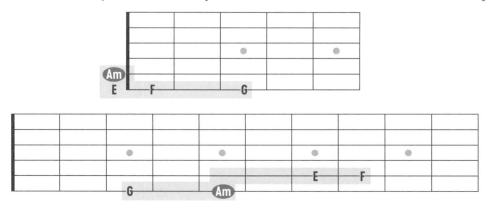

i–♭III–♭VII (or ♭III–♭VII–i)

This one has a Southern rock flair to it and has been used in more than one Lynyrd Skynyrd song, not to mention those by countless other bands.

There's no quiz for this chapter—I told you it was the fun chapter!

Chapter 9 Review

- The term *root* is usually applied to a chord, whereas the term *tonic* is usually applied to a scale or a key.
- Roman numerals are assigned to the chords of a key to quickly outline chord progressions—uppercase for major chords and lowercase for minor chords.
- The formula for chords built from the notes of a major scale is: major–minor–minor–major–major–minor–diminished.
- The v chord in a minor key is usually replaced with a major chord to create a stronger resolution to the tonic (i) chord.

AFTERWORD

Well, that does it! Congratulations for sticking to it until the end. If you've come this far, you've no doubt expanded your knowledge of music theory as it relates to the guitar by leaps and bounds. There's still much to learn, of course—I didn't want to scare anyone off by trying to cram everything in one book—and I recommend continuing your pursuit of knowledge if you're still thirsty for more.

In parting, I'd like to encourage you to keep investigating. Keep looking and listening for patterns. If you hear something that reminds you of something else, find out what it is and why. If you don't like something, look/listen more closely to reveal exactly what it is that you don't like. Do the same for sounds that you do like. The more practiced you become at dissecting things and seeing how they work, the easier it will be for you to put things together in ways that you like! Best of luck, and enjoy the journey.

APPENDIX

Fretboard Note Chart

Chapter 1 Quiz Answers

A. 2.

3.

4.

B. 2.

3.

4.

C. 2. B   3. C   4. E

Chapter 2 Quiz Answers

A. 2.

3.

4.

5.

6.

B. 2. WS   3. WS   4. WS   5. HS   6. HS

C. 2. C♯ or D♭   3. A♯ or B♭   4. D♯ or E♭

Chapter 3 Quiz Answers

A. 2.

3.

4.

5.

6.

B. 2. m3   3. M3   4. m3   5. M3   6. m3

C. 2.
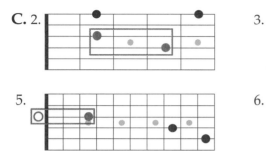
3.

4.
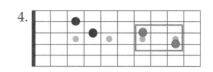

5.
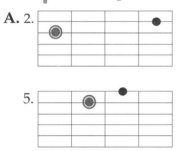
6.

Chapter 4 Quiz Answers

A. 2.
3.
4.

5.
6.

B. 2. ♭5   3. ♯5   4. ♭5   5. P5   6. ♭5

C. 2. aug   3. dim   4. dim   5. aug   6. aug

Chapter 5 Quiz Answers

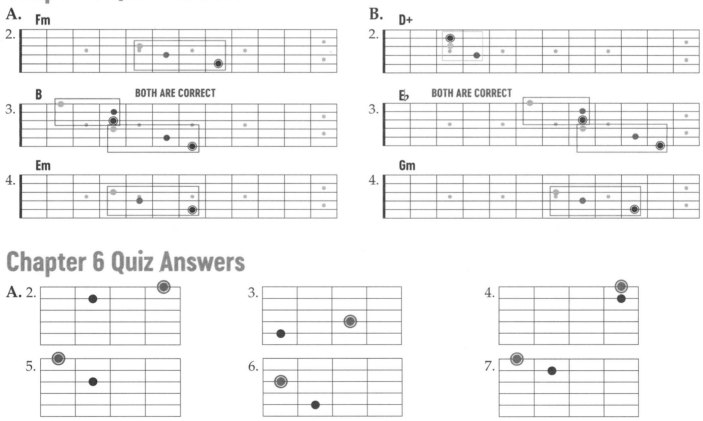

Chapter 6 Quiz Answers

A. 2.
3.
4.

5.
6.
7.

8.

B. 2. P4   3. M6   4. m6 or a5   5. m6 or a5   6. a4 or d5

C. 2. Augmented – 1st inv.   3. Minor – root pos.   4. Augmented – 2nd inv.   5. Diminished – 1st inv.
6. Major – 1st inv.   7. Diminished – 2nd inv.   8. Minor – 1st inv.

Chapter 7 Quiz Answers

A. 2. M7   3. M7   4. M7   5. m7   6. M7

B. 2.    3. 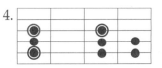   4.

C. 1. whole   2. perfect 4th   3. whole   4. major 7th

Chapter 8 Quiz Answers

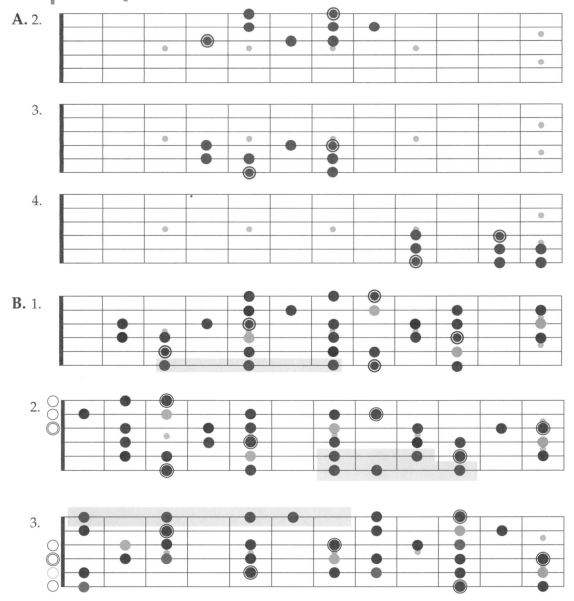